CATALOGUE OF BOOKS

CONTAINED IN THE

LIBRARY OF THE AMERICAN BIBLE SOCIETY,

EMBRACING

EDITIONS OF THE HOLY SCRIPTURES IN VARIOUS LANGUAGES,

AND

OTHER BIBLICAL AND MISCELLANEOUS WORKS.

AMERICAN BIBLE SOCIETY'S PRESS,
ASTOR PLACE, NEW YORK.

1855.

CONTENTS.

*** The *English* versions of the Holy Scriptures are arranged ***chronologically;*** those in *Foreign* languages, *alphabetically*, in the order of their respective languages. All the other works are arranged alphabetically under the names of the *Authors*, except those which are *Anonymous*, which are placed in chronological order.

Note.—The books contained in this Catalogue have been mostly *presented* to the Society by its friends.

NOTICE.

Two important books, not having been received when the Catalogue was drawn up, were omitted in the main body, and are placed here. The first work properly belongs to page 5, and the second to page 63.

1549.—THE BIBLE, whych is all the Holy Scripture: in whych are contained the Olde and Newe Testament, truelye and purely translated into Englishe by Thomas Matthew, 1537, and now imprinted in the Yeare of oure Lorde M.D.XLIX., by Thomas Raynolde and William Hyll, dwelling in Paule's Churche Yeard.—Fol., London, 1549. In Black Letter. (G.)

BIBLIA SACRA LATINA cum postillis Nicolai de Lyra.—6 vols. fol., Argentinae, 1501. (G.)

The Prologue commences thus: "In nomine sanctae Trinitatis: incipit prologus primus venerabilis fratris Nicolai de Lyra ordinis seraphici Francisci: de comendatione Sacre Scripture in generali." Nicolai was born at Lyre, in Normandy, in the 13th century, of Jewish parents. He embraced Christianity at an early age, and entered the order of Franciscans at Verneuil in 1291. He was distinguished as a Hebrew scholar, and wrote several works defending Christianity against the attacks of Jewish writers. Walchius says of him: "In explaining the literal sense of the Holy Scriptures he excelled most of his cotemporaries. On those passages of the New Testament which derive illustration from Jewish antiquities, he has thrown considerable light. Unshackled by the authority of the Fathers, he thought for himself, as his works sufficiently discover." The labours of Nicolai de Lyra are regarded as having led to the Reformation. It has been said,

"Si Lyra non lyrasset,
Lutherus non saltasset;"

which was afterwards translated thus:

"If Lyra had not *harped* on profanation,
Luther had not *planned* the Reformation."

HOLY SCRIPTURES.

ENGLISH VERSIONS.

1526.—**The Newe Testament.** MDXXVI. The New Testament of our Lord and Saviour Jesus Christ; published in 1526. Being the first translation (of the New Testament) from the Greek into English, by that eminent scholar and martyr, William Tyndale. Reprinted verbatim; with a memoir of his life and writings, by George Offor; together with the proceedings and correspondence of Henry VIII., Sir T. Moore, and Lord Cromwell.—Imp. 8vo, (Bagster), London, 1836. (G.)

1535.—Biblia, The Bible; that is, the Holy Scripture of the Olde and New Testament, faithfully and truly translated into English, MDXXXV. S. Paul, II. Thess. III.: Praie for us, that the worde of God maie haue fre passage and be glorified, zct. Reprinted from the copy in the Library of the Duke of Sussex.—4to, (Bagster), London, 1838. (G.)

This is a *reprint* of the Bible translated by Myles Coverdale. The title is in Black; the text was originally printed in a Gothic type. On the reverse of the last leaf of the New Testament is, "Prynted in the yeare of oure Lorde MDXXXV., and fynished the fourth daye of October." This version was the first entire Bible printed in English. It is dedicated to Henry VIII. by the translator. The title is inserted in a curious historical woodcut. When the work was completed it was presented to the king, who delivered it to Bishop Gardiner and others to examine; but they were so dilatory in reporting, that the king made a requisition on them for their opinion, to which they replied, "there were many faults in it." "Well," said the king, "but are there any heresies maintained in it?" To which they answered, "None that they could find." "Then, in God's name," added the king, "let it go abroad among our people." [See Cotton's List of Eng. Editions of the Bible, fol. 3, 111. Also, see Bibliotheca Sussexiana, vol. ii., fol. 281.] The original copies had no date or place of publication.

1557.—The Newe Testament of our Lord Jesus Christ, conferred diligently with the Greke, and best approved translations. With the arguments as well before the chapters as for every Boke and Epistle; also diversities of readings, &c., &c.—Reprinted, 12mo, London, 1842. (G.)

This is a fac-simile reprint of the celebrated Genevan Testament, the original edition of which was the first in which the *verses* are distinguished by figures. The translation differs from that which, three years afterwards, was printed at the same place in connection with the Old Testament. The vignette represents *Time* restoring *Truth* from a cave. At the end of the book is this imprint: "Printed by Conrad Badius MDLVII this X of IVNE." [See Cotton, p. 14, 138.]

1572.—THE HOLIE BIBLE, conteyning the Olde Testament and the Newe. Printed by Richard Jugg.—Fol., London, 1572. (G.)

This is the second folio edition of Parker's, or the "Bishops'" Bible; so called, because translated chiefly by bishops of the English Church. The first edition was published in 1568. The second differs somewhat from the first. The Almanac begins with 1572, and ends with 1610. The Calendar has the signs of the Zodiac on the inner margin. Most of the Romish saints are taken away. The woodcut at the beginning of Genesis is different, and is inserted in a frame-work composed of another woodcut. It has less than one fourth the number of engravings that the first edition contained. It has a double version of the Psalms, one in Black letter, which is used in the Prayer Book, the other from the Hebrew in Roman letter. The first edition and this contained portraits on copperplate of Queen Elizabeth, Lord Leicester, and Lord Burleigh, which were not inserted in any subsequent edition, and were not originally added to *every* copy even of these two editions. There is a perfect copy in the Library of Baliol College of the edition of 1572, in which the portraits have never been impressed. Dr. Cotton remarks, that these two editions are very frequently found *robbed* of their portraits; and the present copy must rank either among the neglected or the pilfered ones. It is also otherwise imperfect: the title page is wanting, and much of the preliminary matter. It has, however, the Prologue of Archbishop Cranmer, with his coat of arms in the initial letter (that of Lord Leicester is in the initial to the Book of Joshua), and various woodcuts, as in the first edition. The leaf of the New Testament containing the 13th and portions of the 12th and 14th chapters of John, has been lost, and its place supplied with one from a different edition. An aperture in the leaf containing the 19th chapter of Acts, at the 17th, 18th, and 19th verses, is supplied in MS. With all its imperfections, however, the copy is very rare and valuable. It was the authorized version to be read in public for nearly half a century previous to King James's version, and was the standard for his translators. Anderson states that there were thirty-two editions of this version issued. This copy is in the original *oak* binding, covered with leather. [See Cotton's List, &c., p. 17, 125.]

1575.—HOLIE BIBLE. (The Bishops'.) Printed by J. Judson.—Fol., London, 1575. (G.)

This is a very imperfect copy of one of the later editions of the Bishops' Bible. It was once in the possession of Sir William Pepperell, and the autograph on the inside of the cover is supposed to be his.

1578.—THE FOUR GOSPELS (Black letter), being a remnant of the New Testament.—32mo, 1578. (G.)

Title page gone, and all the rest of the volume after the first leaf of the Book of Acts. It is not mentioned by Cotton or Pettigrew. An Almanac, with lessons for morning and evening prayer, precedes Matthew.

1580.—THE HOLY BIBLE, &c. Imprinted by Christopher Barker, &c.—4to, London, 1580. (G.)

Not mentioned by Cotton. The text is in Black letter, the marginal readings, &c., in Roman. It has no Apocrypha. Nearly all the preliminary matter and the title page to the Old Testament are wanting. It contains arguments to the books, and at the end of the Old Testament, "The Summe of the whole Scripture of the Bookes of the Olde and Newe Testament," and "Certaine Questions and Answeres touching the Doctrine of Predestination, the use of God's Word and Sacraments," &c. At the end of the New Testament are "Two right profitable and fruitfull Concordances, or large and ample tables alphabeticall," &c., &c. Altogether, it is a curious volume.

1580.—THE NEW TESTAMENT, from the Latin of Theo. Beza; with short expositions by Villerius; Englished by Tomson.—12mo, London, 1580. (G.)

Imperfect—beginning with Luke, vi., 11, and ending with Rev., xiii., 5.

1583.—THE BIBLE. (Genevan.) Translated according to the Ebrew and Greeke, &c., with most profitable annotations, &c. Imprinted by Chr. Barker, Printer to the Queen's most excellent Maiestie, &c. —Fol., London, 1583. (G.)

This version contains a Poem on the value of the Bible; various and curious woodcuts, maps, diagrams, &c., and is a perfect copy, and a beautiful specimen of Black letter type. The Book of Psalms, as well as the Old and New Testaments, have each an engraved title page. The first Genevan edition was that of 1560, which contained an epistle to the queen, and another to the reader, not inserted in the subsequent edition. Upwards of fifty editions of this version were printed during thirty years. Mr. Cotton says its notes were retained in some of the editions of King James's version as late as 1715. "This Bible," says Mr. Pettigrew, "is well known as the 'BREECHES BIBLE,' from the translation of Gen., iii., 7. The Genevan translation is unquestionably the first to *print* it so, but I find that it is used in a MS. Wicliff Bible now in the British Museum, in 2 vols., fol. The passage reads thus: 'And whan yei knewen yat ya were nakid, ya sewiden ye levis of a fig tre, and madin brechis to hem self.'" [See Bib. Sussexiana, p. 307.] The passage in this edition of the Genevan version differs from Wicliff, and reads thus: "And they knew that they were naked, and they sewed figge tree leaves together, and made themselves breeches."

1595.—THE BIBLE. (Genevan.) Imprinted by the deputies of Chr. Barker, &c.—4to, London, 1595. (G.)

This edition also contains the Poem, and many of the plates and maps of that of 1583, in smaller size. It is in Roman letter. At the end is an imperfect copy of Sternhold and Hopkins's Psalms, in Black letter.

1596.—THE BIBLE. (Black letter. Title in Roman.) Imprinted by the deputies of Chr. Barker, &c.—4to, London, 1596. (G.)

Not found in the Sussex Catalogue. Dr. Cotton mentions but three copies of it. This copy is imperfect in its preliminaries; and the whole of Genesis, and the first ten chapters of Exodus, are supplied from the authorized edition of 1613, being of the same letter. After the New Testament there are "Two right profitable and fruitfull Concordances, &c., alphabeticall," &c., with a Preface by Robert F. Herrey, dated 1578; after which is a nearly perfect copy of Sternhold and Hopkins's Psalms, set to music, with a recommendatory preface to the reader, as a work whereby he may "the more easily come to the knowledge of perfect solefayeing." After the Psalms are the Ten Commandments, the Lord's Prayer, the Creed, and a Prayer to the Holy Ghost, all in metre, and set to music, together with the benediction, a lamentation, and a thanksgiving, with a closing prayer, commencing thus:

"Preserve us, Lord, by thy deare Worde;
from Pope and Turke defend us, Lorde,
which both would thrust out of his throne,
our Lord Jesus Christ, thy deare Sonne."

1599.—THE BIBLE. (Genevan version.) Imprinted by the deputies of Chr. Barker.—4to, London, 1599. (G.)

An imperfect copy. Title page of the Old and the New Testament wanting; also the text of the Old Testament to 2 Chron., xxii., and of the New Testament to Matt., vi., and all after 1 Cor., x. It has no Apocrypha, and no authority for the date, except a MS. note by its former owner. Of this edition Dr. Cotton says, "The impression was probably a very large one, as it appears to be the most common of all the Genevan editions."

1601.—THE BIBLE. (Beza's translation.) Imprinted by Robert Barker, Printer, &c., &c.—4to, London, 1601. (G.)

An imperfect copy. Title page of the Old Testament and first four chapters of Genesis wanting.

1605.—THE BIBLE. (Black letter.) Imprinted by Robert Barker, &c.—4to, London, 1605. (G.)

A similar edition to that of 1596. This copy also is imperfect. Title pages gone. The only interest that attaches to this copy is in some MS. verses prefixed to the volume, with the following note appended: "This Bible was brought to America by one of the New England Pilgrims. The accident which befell it, and the manner in which it was repaired, are faithfully described in the following verses," &c. Dated Norwich, 1828.

1610.—THE BIBLE; that is, the Holy Scriptures contained in the Old and New Testament; translated according to the Ebrew and Greeke, &c. Imprinted by Robert Barker, Printer, &c.—Fol., London, 1610. (G.)

This is one of the last editions of the Genevan version, previous to that of King James. But one copy of it is mentioned by Dr. Cotton, that of the Earl of Bridgewater. The Old and New Testaments and the Psalms have each an engraved title page.

1610.—THE HOLY BIBLE, faithfully translated into English, &c., with arguments of the books and chapters, annotations, tables, and other helps for the better understanding of the text, &c. By the English College of Doway, &c.—2 vols. 4to, Doway, 1610. (G.)

This is a copy of the first edition of the Doway Bible. It contains the Old Testament and the Apocrypha. The New Testament was published at Rheims, A.D. 1582, and is not included in these volumes, which seem to have belonged to different sets.

1610.—THE HOLY SCRIPTURES, &c., translated according to the Ebrew and Greeke, &c., with most profitable annotations, &c., by Theodore Beza. Englished by L. Tomson. Imprinted by Robert Barker.—Fol., London, 1610. In Black letter. (G.)

1611.—THE HOLY BIBLE, conteyning the Old Testament and the New. Newly translated out of the original tongues, and with the former translations diligently compared and revised, by His Maiestie's speciall commandement. Appointed to be read in churches. Imprinted at London by Robert Barker, &c., Anno Domini MDCXI.—Imp. 4to, reprinted at the University Press, Oxford, 1833. (G.)

This is an exact reprint, page for page, in Roman letter, of the authorized version published in the year 1611, in Black letter, folio, with the Translators' Preface, the Apocrypha, and the Dedication to the King. It is collated with a subsequent edition of 1613, and a list of various readings appended. The reprint of the text is so exactly literatim as to retain even the manifest errors of the press.

1612.—The Holy Bible, conteyning the Old Testament and the New, &c., &c. (King James's version.) Imprinted by R. Barker, &c. —4to, London, 1612. (G.)

This edition is in Roman letter, and very scarce. No copy is mentioned by Pettigrew, and but one by Cotton. The title is arranged in the form of a heart, with broad woodcut borders, containing the names of the twelve patriarchs and of the apostles. This copy is imperfect, wanting the title page to the Old Testament and all the preliminary matter.

1612.—The Holy Bible, &c. (King James's version.) Imprinted by Robert Barker, &c.—4to, London, 1612. (G.)

The arrangement of the title, &c., is similar to the edition last named. All the preliminary matter, the title page to the Old Testament, the first twenty-one chapters of Genesis, the Apocrypha, part of the last chapter of Revelation, and a portion of Sternhold and Hopkins's Psalms, are wanting. It is also otherwise mutilated. It seems to be a corrected edition of the preceding.

1613.—The Holy Bible, &c. (King James's version.) Imprinted by Robert Barker, &c., &c.—Fol., London, 1613. (G.)

It contains the Translators' Preface and the Dedication, with the usual preliminary Calendar, Almanac, Tables, &c., with thirty-four pages of genealogies. The text is in Black letter.

1613.—The Holy Bible, &c., &c. (King James's version.) Imprinted by R. Barker, &c.—4to, London, 1613. (G.)

This is similar in its arrangement to the folio edition of the same date. The New Testament bears date 1614. The text is in small Black letter. It contains the Dedication, the Translators' Address, and Speed's Genealogies, with a curious map and description of Canaan. All the matter, except the text, is in Roman letter; the marginal readings in Italic.

1615.—The Bible. (Genevan version.) Imprinted by Robert Barker, &c.—4to, London, 1615. (G.)

This edition is similar to the 4to of 1612. The text is in Black letter, the notes in Roman.

1617.—The Holy Bible, &c., &c. (King James's version.) Imprinted by Robert Barker, &c.—Fol., London, 1617. (G.)

1628.—The Holy Bible, &c. (King James's version.) Imprinted by Bonham, Norton, and J. Bill, &c.—4to, London, 1628. (G.)

1629.—The Holy Bible, &c. (King James's version.) Imprinted by Thomas and John Buck, Printers to the University of Cambridge.—Fol., Anno Dom. 1629. (G.)

1630.—The Holy Bible, &c. (King James's version.)

Printed by Thomas and John Buck, &c.—4to, Cambridge, Anno Dom. 1630. (G.)

This edition is in Black letter. The title page of the Old Testament is wanting; that of the New is inserted in the form of a heart, with a heavy woodcut border, containing the names of the patriarchs and apostles. Prefixed are chronological charts, maps, the Book of Common Prayer, &c., and at the end Sternhold and Hopkins's Psalms.

1630.—The Holy Bible, &c. (King James's version.) Imprinted by Robert Barker, &c.—4to, London, 1630. (G.)

This copy is in Roman letter, and in red ruling. The title page to the Old Testament, the Apocrypha, &c., are wanting. It has Sternhold and Hopkins's Psalms at the end.

1630.—The Holy Bible, &c. (King James's version.) Imprinted by Robert Barker and John Bill, Printers, &c.—8vo, London, 1630. (G.)

The title page to the Old Testament is wanting.

1630.—The Holy Bible, &c. (King James's version.) Printed by Robert Barker and the assigns of John Bill.—8vo, London, 1630. (G.)

The title pages are wanting, and the volume is otherwise imperfect. The date and imprint are at the end of the volume. It has tables of chronology prefixed.

1632.—The Holy Bible, &c. (King James's version.) Printed by R. Barker and Assignees of John Bill.—8vo, London, 1632. (G.)

It is somewhat mutilated.

1637.—The Holy Bible, &c. (King James's version.) Printed by Thomas Buck and Roger Daniel, Printers to the University.—4to, Cambridge, 1637. (G.)

This edition is in Roman type. The Prayer Book precedes the Old Testament. The title page of the New Testament is wanting.

1639.—The Holy Bible, &c. (King James's version.) Printed by Robert Barker and Assignees of John Bill.—8vo, London, 1639. (G.)

This copy is in red ruling.

1639.—The Holy Bible, &c. Printed by R. Barker, Printer, &c., and by the Assignees of J. Bill.—4to, London, 1639. (G.)

In Black letter. The Prayer Book is prefixed, and a Concordance by J. Downame appended, with Sternhold and Hopkins's Psalms, and forms of prayer.

1640.—The Holy Bible, &c. (King James's version.) Printed by R. Barker and Assignees of J. Bill.—8vo, London, 1640. (G.)

1642.—The Holy Bible, &c., as above.—8vo, London, 1642. (G.)

This copy has lost part of the Apocrypha and all the New Testament. It is in red ruling.

1648.—The Holy Bible, &c. (King James's version.) Printed by R. Barker.—12mo, London, 1648. (G.)

It is without the Apocrypha.

1653.—The Holy Bible, &c. (Field's Pearl edition.) —32mo, London, 1653. (G.)

The title page to the Old Testament is lost, and that of the New Testament transposed to its place in rebinding. This copy is in red ruling, and bound in morocco; and, according to tradition, was once in the possession of the poet Milton.

1657.—The Holy Bible, &c. (King James's version.) Printed by John Field.—12mo, London, 1657. (G.)

It has no Apocrypha.

1658.—The Holy Bible, &c. (King James's version.) Printed by John Field, one of His Highness's Printers.—24mo, London, 1658. (G.)

No Apocrypha. A correct and beautiful edition, and has sometimes been sold at £4.

1660.—The Holy Bible, &c. (King James's version.) Printed by Henry Hills and John Field.—12mo, London, 1660. (G.)

It is without the Apocrypha. The title page to the Old Testament is wanting.

1660.—The Holy Bible, &c. (King James's version.) Printed by John Field.—12mo, London, 1660. (G.)

It is without the Apocrypha. This copy is in red ruling, and is a beautiful volume.

1660.—The Holy Bible, &c. (King James's version.) Printed by John Field.—Fol., Cambridge, 1660. (G.)

A fine edition on large paper.

1661.—The Holy Bible, &c. (King James's version.) Printed by John Field, Printer to the University.—8vo, Cambridge, 1661. (G.)

Without the Apocrypha.

1666.—The Holy Bible, &c. (King James's version.) Printed by John Field.—4to, Cambridge, 1666. (G.)

In Roman letter. The title page to the Old Testament is wanting. It has no Apocrypha. At the end is a Concordance, part of which is wanting.

1668.—The Holy Bible, &c. (King James's version.) Printed by John Field.—4to, Cambridge, 1668. (G.)

In Roman letter. This edition has no Apocrypha, and no preliminary matter, except the Dedication. Appended is a copy of the Psalms in metre, with a title, representing it as "more plain, smooth, and agreeable" than any previous versions; and as "allowed by the General Assembly of the Kirk of Scotland, and appointed to be sung in congregations and families."

1671.—THE HOLY BIBLE, &c. (King James's version.) Printed by the Assigns of J. Bill, and Christopher Barker, &c.—8vo, London, 1671. (G.)

In Roman letter. "In the Savoy." This edition is accompanied by the Prayer Book and Sternhold and Hopkins's Psalms.

1713.—THE HOLY BIBLE, &c. (King James's version.) Printed by John Baskett and the Assigns of Thomas Newcomb and Henry Hills.—12mo, London, 1713. (G.)

This edition is in red ruling, and has no Apocrypha.

1726.—THE HOLY BIBLE, &c. (King James's version.) Printed by J. Baskett.—4to, Oxford, 1726. (G.)

This edition has the Prayer Book and metrical Psalms, and is embellished with numerous engravings.

1730.—THE HOLY BIBLE, &c. (King James's version.) "Printed in the year MDCCXXX."—4to. (G.)

The date of the New Testament is 1728, and is without the name of its place of publication. The Prayer Book, which is prefixed, bears date, LONDON, 1728.

1730.—THE NEW TESTAMENT, &c., according to the ancient Latin edition, with critical remarks, &c., from the French of Father Simon. By William Webster, curate, &c.—2 vols. 4to, London, 1730. (G.)

1739.—THE HOLY BIBLE, &c. (King James's version.) Printed by John Baskett, Printer to the University.—12mo, Oxford, 1739. (G.)

It has the Scotch Psalms in verse, but no Apocrypha.

1747.—THE HOLY BIBLE, &c. (King James's version.) University Press.—2 vols. 4to, Oxford, 1747. (G.)

This copy is interleaved, probably for its owner's use, as it has various MS. notes.

1749.—THE NEW TESTAMENT, &c., translated out of the Latin Vulgate, diligently compared with the Greek, and first published by the English College of Rheims, Anno 1582. Newly revised, &c., with annotations for clearing up modern controversies in religion, &c.—12mo, Rheims, 1749. (G.)

This is the authorized version of the Romish Church.

1754.—THE NEW TESTAMENT, with explanatory notes by Rev. John Westley, A.M.—8vo, London, 1754.—(G).

1761.—THE HOLY BIBLE, &c. (King James's version.) Printed by Thomas Baskett.—4to, London, 1761. (G.)

1764.—THE HOLY BIBLE, illustrated and explained, &c., together with the Books of the Apocrypha. Embellished with 110 engravings, &c. By Rev. John Butley.—2 vols. 4to, London, 1764. (G.)

1769.—The Holy Bible, &c. (King James's version.) Printed by T. Wright and W. Gill, Printers to the University.—2 vols. 4to, Oxford, 1769. (G.)

1769.—The Holy Bible, &c. (King James's version.) Printed by T. Wright and W. Gill, &c.—3 vols. 4to, Oxford, 1769. (G.)

This is generally entitled "The Standard Edition." It was corrected by Rev. Dr. Blaney, under the direction of the vice-chancellor, and delegates of the Clarendon Press at Oxford. The punctuation was carefully revised, the words in Italic were compared with the Hebrew and Greek originals, running titles corrected, &c., &c., and 30,495 new marginal references inserted, &c. A simultaneous folio edition was printed with this, and in overrunning the folio into the 4to size, the words "AT ALL IN THEE" were omitted from Rev., xviii., 22. The first editions were issued in 1762. [Gent.'s Mag., vol. xxxix., p. 517.]

1782.—The Holy Bible, &c. (King James's version.) Printed and sold by R. Aitken, at Pope's Head, three doors above the Coffee House in Market Street.—12mo, Philadelphia, 1782. (G.)

The New Testament bears date 1781. This is a copy of the edition of the Bible reported to Congress by the committee previously appointed on the subject, and respecting which the following resolution was adopted:

"*Resolved*, That the United States, in Congress assembled, highly approve the pious and laudable undertaking of Mr. Aitken, as subservient to the interest of religion, as well as an instance of the progress of arts in this country; and being satisfied, from the above report, of his care and accuracy in the execution of the work, they *recommend this edition of the Bible to the inhabitants of the United States;* and hereby authorize him to publish this recommendation in the manner he shall think proper.

"CHA. THOMSON, Secretary."

The report and the recommendation are prefixed to the Bible, and are a standing memento that the fathers of our country deemed the circulation of the Bible important to its political as well as religious interests.

1785.—The New Testament, &c. (King James's version.) Printed at the Clarendon Press by W. Jackson, &c.—12mo, Oxford, 1785. (G.)

1790.—The Holy Bible, &c., (King James's version), with the Apocrypha and a Concordance.—4to, Trenton, 1790. (G.)

1791.—The Holy Bible, &c., with an Index. (King James's version.) Printed by Isaiah Thomas.—2 vols. fol., Worcester, (Mass.), 1791. (G.)

This is the first folio Bible printed in the United States. It contains the Apocrypha, and is illustrated with engravings. Mr. Thomas issued a quarto edition during the same year.

1791.—The Holy Bible, &c. (King James's version.) Printed by Isaac Collins.—4to, Trenton, 1791. (G.)

This copy contains an Index and Concordance. The title page to the Old Testament is wanting.

1791.—A new Translation of the New Testament, with a Preface and Notes, by Gilbert Wakefield, B.A.—3 vols. 8vo, 1791. (G.)

This translation is tinctured by his creed.

1792.—The Holy Bible, &c. (King James's version.) Printed by Hodge and Campbell.—4to, New York, 1792. (G.)

It is printed on English paper, with an Index, &c., and the metrical Psalms. The Apocrypha is in a smaller type than that of the sacred text.

1792.—The Self-Interpreting Bible, with marginal references, notes, &c., by Rev. John Brown.—Fol., New York, 1792. (G.)

1796.—The Holy Bible, &c., (King James's version), with the Apocrypha and marginal references. Printed by Berriman & Co.—Fol., Philadelphia, 1796. (G.)

1802.—The Holy Bible, with a Preface and Notes, &c. Printed in the ancient form, preserving all the uses and avoiding the disadvantages of the modern division into chapters and verses. By John Reeves. —9 vols. 8vo, London, 1802. (G.)

1803.—The Holy Bible, &c., (King James's version), with references. Printed by Sir D. Hunter Blair and J. Bruce, Printers to the King.—12mo, Edinburgh, 1803. (G.)

In this edition the chapter heads are much abbreviated.

1808.—The Old and New Testaments, digested and illustrated by way of Question and Answer, from the writings of the most eminent Historians and Commentators. First American edition.—8vo, Baltimore, 1808. (G.)

1812.—The Holy Bible, &c. Stereotyped for the Philadelphia Bible Society by T. Rutt, Shacklewell, London.—12mo, Philadelphia, 1812. (G.)

1813.—The Holy Bible, &c. (King James's version.) Printed by George Eyre and Andrew Strahan.—4to, London, 1813. (G.)

This was formerly the Pulpit Bible of the First Presbyterian Church, Monrovia, Africa. Being sent here for repair, it was retained, and its place supplied with a new one in 1841.

1813.—The Holy Bible, &c. (King James's version.) Printed for George Eyre and Andrew Strahan.—4to, London, 1813. (G.)

"In 1806 Eyre and Strahan published a quarto edition of the Bible, superior, in point of accuracy, to the 'Standard Edition' of 1769. This edition of 1813 is considered equally accurate with that of 1806. It has been recommended by the General Convention of the Protestant Episcopal Church of the United States, to be adopted as their standard edition." [Lownde's Brit. Lib., 1839.]

1814.—The Holy Bible, &c. Printed by Eyre and Strahan for the British and Foreign Bible Society.—12mo, London, 1814. (G.)

1815.—THE HOLY BIBLE, &c. (King James's version.) D. and G. Bruce.—12mo, New York, 1815. (G.)

1815.—THE HOLY BIBLE, &c. Printed by Eyre and Strahan for the British and Foreign Bible Society.—8vo, London, 1815. (G.)

1816.—THE HOLY BIBLE, &c., with the Apocrypha, and Canne's Notes, Brown's Concordance, &c.: embellished with maps and plates. Collins & Co.—4to, New York, 1816. (G.)

First stereotyped 4to published in the United States.

1816.—THE NEW TESTAMENT, &c. Stereotyped for the Philadelphia Bible Society by T. Rutt, Shacklewell.—8vo, London, 1816. (G.)

1816.—THE HOLY BIBLE, &c. (King James's version.) Stereotyped by E. and J. White for the New York Bible Society.—12mo, New York, 1816. (G.)

1816.—THE HOLY BIBLE, &c. Stereotyped for the Philadelphia Bible Society by T. Rutt, Shacklewell.—8vo, London, 1816. (G.)

1817.—THE HOLY BIBLE, &c., with the Apocrypha, and Canne's Notes and References, &c. Collins & Co.—4to, New York, 1817. (J.)

1817.—THE HOLY BIBLE, &c. (King James's version.) Stereotyped by E. and J. White for the American Bible Society.—8vo, New York, 1817. (G.)

1817.—THE HOLY BIBLE, &c. (King James's version.) Stereotype edition. Eyre and Strahan for the British and Foreign Bible Society.—2 vols. royal 8vo, London, 1817. In boards. (J.)

1817.—THE HOLY BIBLE, &c. (King James's version.) Printed by Eyre and Strahan for the British and Foreign Bible Society.—8vo, London, 1817. (G.)

1817.—THE NEW TESTAMENT in an improved version, upon the basis of Archbishop Newcome's new translation, with a corrected text, and notes critical and explanatory, &c. Fourth edition. Published by the Unitarian Society for promoting Christian Knowledge, &c.—8vo, London, 1817. (G.)

1818.—THE HOLY BIBLE, &c. (King James's version.) Printed by Eyre and Strahan for the British and Foreign Bible Society.—Ruby, 24mo, London, 1818. (G.)

1818.—THE HOLY BIBLE, &c. Printed by Eyre and Strahan for the British and Foreign Bible Society.—Small Pica, 8vo, London, 1818. (G.)

1819.—THE NEW TESTAMENT, &c. Stereotyped by E. and J. White for the American Bible Society.—8vo, New York, 1819. Two copies. (G.)

1819.—The Holy Bible, &c. Printed for the Kentucky Auxiliary Bible Society.—12mo, Lexington, 1819. (G.)

1820.—The Holy Bible, &c., (King James's version), arranged for a course of family reading; to which is annexed, "The Family Guide to the Holy Scriptures, upon the plan of the late Bishop Porteus." Printed for the Porteusian Society.—12mo, London, 1820. (G.)

1821.—The Holy Bible, &c. (King James's version.) —Minion, 8vo, Oxford, 1821. (G.)

1821.—The Holy Bible, &c. (King James's version.) Stereotyped by E. and J. White for the American Bible Society.—8vo, New York, 1821. (G.)

1821.—Another copy as above (imperfect).—12mo, New York, 1821. (G.)

1821.—The Holy Bible, &c. Printed by the New York Auxiliary Bible and Common Prayer Book Society.—12mo, New York, 1821. (G.)

1822.—The New Testament, &c. Stereotyped by J. Howe, New York. Printed at Treadwell's power press, Boston.—12mo, Boston, 1822. (G.)

1823.—The New Testament, &c. By A. Paul for the American Bible Society.—12mo, New York, 1823. (G.)

1823.—The English version of the Polyglott Bible, containing the Old and New Testaments: with a copious and original selection of references to parallel and illustrative passages, &c. Printed for Samuel Bagster.—Cap 8vo, London, 1823. (G.)

1823.—The Holy Bible, &c.—12mo, Philadelphia, 1823. (G.)

1823. See Kneeland's version of this date under *Foreign Languages*.

1824.—The New Testament, &c. Stereotyped by A. Chandler for the American Bible Society.—8vo, New York, 1824. (G.)

1824.—The New Testament, &c. Stereotyped for the Philadelphia Bible Society.—18mo, Philadelphia, 1824. (G.)

1825.—The Holy Bible, &c. Printed by Eyre and Strahan for the British and Foreign Bible Society.—8vo, London, 1825. (G.)

1825.—The New Testament, &c. Printed by Blair and Bruce for the Hibernian Bible Society.—12mo, Edinburgh, 1825. (G.)

1826.—The Holy Bible, &c. (King James's version.) A. Paul for the American Bible Society.—18mo, New York, 1826. (G.)

1826.—The Reference Bible, &c., with a Key-sheet of

Questions, geographical, historical, doctrinal, and practical, &c., by Henry Wilbur.—2 vols. 12mo, Boston, 1826. (G.)

1827.—The Holy Bible. (King James's version.) Eyre and Strahan for the British and Foreign Bible Society.—12mo, London, 1827. Two copies. (G.)

1827.—The New Testament, &c. American Bible Society.—12mo, New York, 1827. (G.)

1827.—The New Testament, &c. Eyre and Strahan for the British and Foreign Bible Society.—Brevier, 12mo, London, 1827. (G.)

1828.—The Holy Bible, &c. (King James's version.) Printed by Sir D. Hunter Blair and M. S. Bruce, Printers to the King.—12mo, Edinburgh, 1828. (G.)

With references, but without chapter heads or running titles.

1828.—The Holy Bible, &c. (King James's version.) Printed by Collingwood & Co.—Minion, 12mo, Oxford, 1828. (G.)

This edition is printed in paragraphs, in one column, without chapter heads or head lines to the columns. The numbers of the chapters and verses are placed in the margin.

1828.—The Holy Bible, &c. Published by the Methodist Book Concern.—12mo, New York, 1828. (G.)

1828.—The Holy Bible, &c. Printed for the Bible Society by the American Sunday School Union.—12mo, Philadelphia, 1828. (G.)

1829.—The Holy Bible, &c. (King James's version.) Printed by Hunter and Bruce.—2 vols. 16mo, Edinburgh, 1829. (G.)

A fine edition of the Bible, with the metrical Psalms of the Kirk of Scotland.

1829.—The Holy Bible, &c. Hudson and Skinner. —12mo, Hartford, 1829. (G.)

1829.—The New Testament, &c., translated out of the Latin Vulgate, diligently compared with the Greek, and first published by the English College of Rheims, Anno 1582. Newly revised, &c., with annotations for clearing up modern controversies in religion, &c.—12mo, Utica, 1829. (G.)

The authorized version of the Romish Church, approved by Bishop Dubois, &c.

1830.—The Holy Bible, &c. (King James's version.) Stereotyped by Baker and Greele for the American Bible Society.—8vo, New York, 1830. (G.)

1830.—The New Testament, &c., conformed to Griesbach's Greek text.—12mo, Boston, 1830. (G.)

1831.—THE HOLY BIBLE, &c. Published by the Bible Association of Friends in America.—Small Pica, 3 vols. 8vo, Philadelphia, 1831. (G.)

This edition has references, an Index, Tables of Weights, &c., and Brown's Concordance.

1831.—Another copy of the above.—2 vols. 8vo, Philadelphia, 1831. (G.)

1831.—Another copy of the same.—2 vols. 8vo, 1831. (G.)

1831.—THE HOLY BIBLE, &c. Published by the Association of Friends in America.—Small Pica, 8vo, Philadelphia, 1831. (G.)

1838.—THE NEW TESTAMENT, &c. Published as above. —8vo, Philadelphia, 1831. Two copies. (G.)

1831.—THE HOLY BIBLE, &c. Printed, &c., for the British and Foreign Bible Society.—Pica, 4to, London, 1831. (G.)

1831.—THE HOLY BIBLE, &c. Stereotyped by T. Rutt, London, and printed by D. Fanshaw for the American Bible Society.—8vo, New York, 1831. (G.)

1831.—THE HOLY BIBLE, &c. (King James's version.) Printed for the British and Foreign Bible Society.—Small Pica, royal 8vo, Cambridge, 1831. (G.)

With references and marginal readings.

1831.—THE NEW TESTAMENT, &c., with short explanatory notes, references, &c., in a centre column. Illustrated with maps. Bagster.—32mo, London, 1831. (G.)

This is called THE POLYMICRIAN New Testament.

1832.—THE HOLY BIBLE, &c. Printed by Eyre and Strahan for the British and Foreign Bible Society.—Nonpareil, 12mo, London, 1832. (G.)

With references.

1833.—THE HOLY BIBLE, &c. Stereotyped by James Connor, and printed and published by Edward Sanderson.—12mo, Elizabethtown, 1833. (G.)

1833.—THE HOLY BIBLE, &c., in the common version, with amendments of the language by Noah Webster, LL.D.—8vo, New Haven, 1833. (G.)

1833.—THE VILLAGE TESTAMENT, &c., with notes, original and selected, &c., by Rev. William Patton.—12mo, New York, 1833. (G.)

1833.—THE NEW TESTAMENT. (Rhemish.) Printed by Williams.—12mo, Utica, 1833. (G.)

1834.—The New Testament, &c. Printed for the British and Foreign Bible Society.—Brevier, 12mo, Cambridge, 1834. (G.)

1834.—The Holy Bible, &c., arranged in paragraphs and parallelisms, with philological and explanatory annotations, by T. W. Coit, D.D.—12mo, Cambridge, 1834. (G.)

1835.—The New Testament, &c. Printed at the University Press for the British and Foreign Bible Society.—English, 8vo, Oxford, 1835. (G.)

1836.—The New Testament, &c. Published by the Bible Association of Friends in America.—18mo, Philadelphia, 1836. (G.)

1836.—The New Testament, &c., with references.—Edinburgh, 1836. (G.)

1836.—The Holy Bible. (Doway version.)—8vo, New York, 1836. (G.)

1837.—The Holy Bible, &c.—4to, Cambridge, 1837. (J.)

1838.—The Holy Bible, &c., (King James's version), with Canne's Notes and References, Index, Tables, &c.—Fol., Hartford, 1838. (G.)

1838.—The Holy Bible, &c.—Printed by John W. Parker, Printer to the University.—8vo, Cambridge, 1838. (G.)

1838.—The Holy Bible, &c., with references.—Printed by John W. Parker, Printer to the University.—8vo, Cambridge, 1838. (G.)

1838.—The Holy Bible, &c. London edition of R. Barker, 1611. American Bible Society.—18mo, New York, 1838. (G.)

1838.—See 1535.

1839—The Holy Bible, &c., according to the commonly received version. London, R. Barker, 1611. American and Foreign Bible Society.—8vo, New York, 1839. (G.)

1840.—The Holy Bible, &c., with notes, by John Hobart Caunter, B.D.; with maps and 149 engravings.—8vo, London, 1840. (G.)

1841.—The English Hexapla; exhibiting the six important English translations of the New Testament Scriptures, viz.: *Wiclif, Tyndale, Cranmer, Genevan, Anglo-Rhemish, and Authorized*, or King James's, &c., &c., preceded by an historical account of the English translations. Bagster and Sons.—Imp. 4to, London, 1841. (G.)

1841.—The Holy Bible, &c., with references. Printed by Eyre and Spottiswoode for the British and Foreign Bible Society.—Nonpareil, 12mo, London, 1841. (G.)

1841.—The New Testament, &c. Eyre and Strahan for the Naval and Military Bible Society.—12mo, London, 1841. (G.)

1842.—The Holy Bible, &c. Printed by J. Collingwood & Co.—Ruby, 24mo, Oxford, 1842. (G.)

1842.—The Holy Bible, &c., carefully revised and amended; the meaning of the sacred originals being given in accordance with the best translators, and the most approved Hebrew and Greek lexicographers. By several Biblical Scholars.—Royal 8vo, Philadelphia, 1842. (G.)

1844.—The Holy Bible, &c. Printed by J. W. Parker, Printer to the University.—Minion, 8vo, Cambridge, 1844. (G.)

Used in the recent collation.

1844.—The Holy Bible, &c.—4to, Cambridge, 1844. (J.)

1844.—The New Testament, &c., with the Book of Psalms. American Bible Society.—12mo, New York, 1844. (G.)

1844.—The Book of Revelation, in Greek, edited from ancient authorities, with a new English version, and various readings, by Samuel Prideaux Tregelles.—8vo, London, 1844. (G.)

1845.—The Holy Bible, &c. Printed by Peter Brown. —Nonpareil, 12mo, Edinburgh, 1845. (G.)

Used in the recent collation.

1845.—The Holy Bible, &c., (King James's version), with the Psalms of David in Metre, and translations and paraphrases in verse of several passages of Scripture. Printed by Lumsden and Son.—Glasgow, 8vo, 1845. (G.)

1845.—The Holy Bible, &c. Printed by Eyre and Spottiswoode for the British and Foreign Bible Society.—Nonpareil, 12mo, London, 1845. (G).

Used in the recent collation.

1846.—The Holy Bible, &c.—8vo, London, 1846. (G.)

1846.—The New Testament, &c. Printed by Eyre and Spottiswoode for the British and Foreign Bible Society.—Pica, 8vo, London, 1846. (G.)

1846.—The Holy Bible, &c. Printed at the University Press for the British and Foreign Bible Society.—Nonpareil, 12mo, Oxford, 1846. (G.)

1846.—The Holy Bible, &c. Printed at the University Press for the British and Foreign Bible Society.—Minion, 8vo, Oxford, 1846. (G.)

Used in the recent collation.

1847.—The Holy Bible, &c. Printed by Eyre and Spottiswoode for the British and Foreign Bible Society.—English, 4to, London, 1847. (G.)

A beautiful edition.

1847.—The Holy Bible, &c. (King James's version.) Printed at the University Press for the British and Foreign Bible Society.—Nonpareil, 12mo, Oxford, 1847. (G.)

1847.—The Holy Bible, &c. Printed at the American Bible Society's Press.—8vo, New York, 1847. (G.)

1847.—The Holy Bible, &c. Printed at the University Press for the British and Foreign Bible Society.—Pica, 8vo, Oxford, 1847. (G.)

1847.—The New Testament. (Rhemish.) Laidlie.—12mo, New York, 1847. (G.)

1848.—The Holy Bible, &c. Printed at the American Bible Society's Press.—Small Pica, 8vo, New York. 1848. (G.)

With references. Used in the recent collation.

1848.—The Holy Bible, &c. Printed at the University Press for the British and Foreign Bible Society.—Minion, 8vo, Oxford, 1848. (G.)

1848.—The New Testament, &c. (King James's version.) Printed at the University Press for the British and Foreign Bible Society.—Pica, 8vo, Oxford, 1848. (G.)

1848.—The New Testament, &c. (King James's version.) Printed by Eyre and Spottiswoode for the British and Foreign Bible Society.—English, 8vo, London, 1848. (G.)

1849.—The Holy Bible, &c., with references. Printed at the University Press for the British and Foreign Bible Society.—Small Pica, 8vo, Oxford, 1849. (G.)

1849.—The Holy Bible, &c. Printed at the University Press for the British and Foreign Bible Society.—Ruby, 24mo, Oxford, 1849. (G.)

1849.—The Holy Bible, &c. Printed at the University Press for the British and Foreign Bible Society.—Pica, 8vo, Oxford, 1849. (G.)

1849.—The New Testament, &c. (King James's version.) Printed by Eyre and Spottiswoode for the British and Foreign Bible Society.—Pica, 8vo, London, 1849. (G.)

1849.—The New Testament, &c. (King James's version.) Printed at the University Press for the British and Foreign Bible Society.—Pica, 8vo, Oxford, 1849. (G.)

1849.—The Holy Bible, &c. (King James's version.) Printed at the University Press for the British and Foreign Bible Society.—Minion, 8vo, Oxford, 1849. (G.)

1850.—THE NEW TESTAMENT, &c. Printed at the American Bible Society's Press.—Pica, 8vo, New York, 1850. (G.)

1850.—THE HOLY BIBLE, &c. (King James's version.) Printed at the University Press for the British and Foreign Bible Society.—Nonpareil, 12mo, Oxford, 1850. (G.)

1850.—THE HOLY BIBLE, in paragraphs, printed in Phonetic characters, by Frederic Pitman.—8vo, London, 1850. (G.)

1851.—THE HOLY BIBLE, &c. Press of the American Bible Society.—Pica, royal 8vo, New York, 1851. (G.)

1851.—THE NEW TESTAMENT, or the Book of the Holy Gospel of our Lord and our God, Jesus, the Messiah. A literal translation from the Syriac Peshitu version, by James Murdock, D.D.—8vo, New York, 1851. (G.)

1851.—The commonly received version of the New Testament, &c., with SEVERAL HUNDRED EMENDATIONS. Cone and Wyckoff.—8vo, New York, 1851. (G.)

A Baptist translation.

1853.—THE HOLY BIBLE &c. Printed at the University Press for the British and Foreign Bible Society.—Small Pica, 8vo, Oxford, 1853. (G.)

With references. This copy was presented to the American Bible Society by the committee of the British and Foreign Bible Society as a memorial of the "Jubilee Year," which commenced March 7, 1853.

1853.—THE HOLY BIBLE, &c. Press of the American Bible Society.—18mo, New York, 1853. (G.)

1853.—THE SELF-EXPLANATORY REFERENCE BIBLE; or, the Holy Bible, containing the Old and New Testaments, &c., with marginal readings, and original and selected parallel references PRINTED AT LENGTH. R. Carter and Brothers.—8vo, New York, 1853. (G.)

The reference texts, &c., are printed in full in two small columns in the centre of the page.

1854.—THE HOLY BIBLE, &c. Printed by the New York Bible and Common Prayer Book Society.—8vo, New York, 1854. (G.)

1854.—The Book of Psalms. Printed by George E. Eyre and William Spottiswoode for the British and Foreign Bible Society.—Double Pica, 8vo, London, 1854. (G.)

Presented as a memorial of the "Jubilee Year."

ENGLISH VERSIONS WITHOUT DATE.

THE HOLY BIBLE, &c. Printed by Eyre and Strahan for the British and Foreign Bible Society.—8vo, London. (G.)

THE NEW TESTAMENT, &c. Printed for the British and Foreign Bible Society.—Small Pica, 8vo, Cambridge. (G.)

THE HOLY BIBLE, &c. (King James's version.) Printed by Eyre and Strahan for the British and Foreign Bible Society.—12mo, London. (G.)

THE HOLY BIBLE, &c. (King James's version.) Printed by Eyre and Strahan for the British and Foreign Bible Society.—12mo, London. (G.)

THE NEW TESTAMENT, &c.—32mo, Cooperstown, N. Y.—(G.)

THE OLD TESTAMENT AND APOCRYPHA, with a PSALTER. —4to. (G.)

In Black letter. Imperfect, and date unknown. It has no numerical division of verses, nor chapter heads.

THE HOLY BIBLE, &c.—8vo, Cambridge. (G.)

THE HOLY BIBLE, &c. (King James's version.) Printed by Eyre and Strahan for the British and Foreign Bible Society.—Nonpareil, 8vo, London. (G.)

THE NEW TESTAMENT of our Lord and Saviour Jesus Christ, according to the English authorized version. Printed by Richard Clay for the British and Foreign Bible Society.—12mo, London. (G.)

THE HOLY BIBLE. (King James's version.)—4to. (G.)

In Black letter. Very defective. No title pages nor dates. Its contents are from Exodus, 16th chapter, to the third chapter of James, excepting the first four chapters of Matthew, which are wanting.

THE NEW TESTAMENT. (Rhemish version.) Published by F. Lucas.—32mo, Baltimore. (G.)

HOLY SCRIPTURES

IN FOREIGN LANGUAGES.

POLYGLOTTA.

1599.—NOVUM TESTAMENTUM DOM. NOS. JESU CHRISTI; Syriacè, Ebraicè, Graecè, Latinè, Germanicè, Bohemicè, Italicè, Hispanicè, Gallicè, Anglicè, Danicè, Polonicè; studio et labore, ELIAE HUTTERI. *Germani.*—2 vols. fol., Noribergae, 1599. (E.)

This New Testament is in twelve languages. The Hebrew translation is Hutter's, (made by him in one year.) The Syriac is that of Tremellius, of 1569, with additions by Hutter. The Greek is from the ordinary version. The Latin is the Vulgate. The German is Luther's. The Bohemian is from the edition of 1593. The Italian is the Genevan of 1562. The Spanish is that of Cassiodorus Reyna of 1569. The French is the Genevan of 1588. The English is from the Great Bible of 1562. The Danish is from the edition of 1550; and the Polish, that of 1596. This copy contains only the New Testament. Complete copies of the whole Polyglott are very rare. The Old Testament is in four parts and six languages, viz.: Hebrew, Chaldaic, Greek, Latin, German, and Gallic in the first part; the other three parts the same, with the exception of the last-mentioned language, which in Part II. is Italic; Part III. Saxon; and Part IV. Sclavonic. The manner in which the Hebrew in this Polyglott is printed renders it very useful to students; the *radical* letters being printed in full characters, and over the line those that may be wanting in the word. The *serviles* are printed in hollow, or open characters. [See Pettigrew, vol. i., p. 87.]

1657.—BIBLIA SACRA POLYGLOTTA, Complectantia Textus originales, Hebraicos cum Pentat. Samarit., Chaldaicos, Graecos. Versionumque Antiquarum, Samarit., Chaldaic, Lat. Vulg., Aethopic, Graec. Sept., Syriacae, Arabicae, Persicae. Quicquid comparari poterat, &c., ex vetustissimis MSS. undique conquisitis, optimisque exemplaribus impressis, summâ fide collatis, &c., &c. Edidit Brianus Waltonus, S.T.D. Imp. T. Roycroft. —6 vols. fol., London, 1657. (E.)

This is the most valuable edition of the Hebrew Scriptures ever published. It is replete with important critical learning; embraces *nine* different languages, and is generally accompanied by Castell's Lexicon. The portrait of the editor, usually prefixed to the work, is wanting in this copy. It was commenced in 1653, and finished in 1657. "By permission of Oliver Cromwell, the paper for the work was allowed to be imported free of duty, and an honourable notice of the protector was inserted in the preface. Upon the restoration of Charles II., which took place before the Polyglott was completed, Dr. Walton cancelled some of the leaves, and made great alterations. The notice of Cromwell was suppressed. From this circumstance, the two editions are denominated *republican* and *loyal*. Soon after the publication of this work, a papal interdict was issued against it by Alexander VII. Twelve copies are said to have been printed on LARGE PAPER, one of which is in the Library of St. Paul's Cathedral, with the Lexicon on *large paper*. This Polyglott is of the utmost importance to a critic, not only on account of the extracts which it contains from various important manuscripts, but particularly on account of the Oriental versions from which he must collect various readings to the New Testament. The Septuagint version is printed from the edition of Rome in 1587. The Latin is the Vulgate of Clement VIII. The Chaldee paraphrase is more complete than in any former publication. The edition is enriched with prefaces, treatises on weights and measures, geographical charts, and chronological tables. On page forty-eight of the preliminary matter, at the close of the chapter on the Hebrew and Greek idioms, &c., is the remarkable *cancel*, said by Mr. Butler (in his Horae Biblicae, p. 100) to be found in every copy of the Polyglott examined by himself and his friends, though he has heard that *twelve* copies, and twelve only, are without it. The cancel is effected by a reprinted slip of paper pasted over the fourth and fifth directions for determining the sense of Scripture, and the corollary from them, which appear to have been written by a Roman Catholic; and on being observed, were superseded by the reprint above mentioned, which speaks more in the language of a Protestant (High Church) of the Church of England. (Horae Biblicae, vol. i., p. 145.) On the 11th to the 14th pages inclusive of the Prolegomena, are specimens of the Alphabets of the various languages employed in the work, with one of the Chinese. This copy is a *loyal* one, containing Bishop Walton's Dedication to Charles II., which is so rare that Dr. Clarke, when he published his Bibliographical Dictionary, said there was no such Dedication, though he afterwards saw it. Mr. Butler says he had never seen a copy with the Dedication, but Dr. Dibden mentions *seven* copies which contain it. [See Bib. Sussexiana, vol. i., p. 50.]

1710–11.—BIBLIA PENTAPLA, das ist, Die Bücher der Heiligen Schrift, des Alten und Neuen Testaments, nach Fünf-facher Deutscher Verdolmetschung, &c.—3 vols. 4to, Wandsbeck, 1710–11. (F.)

This work contains five different German versions. 1. Caspar Ulenberg's Roman Catholic version; 2. Martin Luther's German version; 3. John Piscator's version of the Reformed Church; 4. The Jewish German version of the Old Testament by Joseph Athias, and of the New Testament by John Henry Keitzen; 5. The authorized version of the Belgic Provinces, or Dutch. To these are added the Apocryphal books of the Old Testament, and several of the Apocryphal epistles. The whole are arranged in five small parallel columns on each page, with an Appendix of Registers of Names, Map of Canaan, &c.

AMERICAN INDIAN.

ABENAQUIS, (Lower Canada.)

THE GOSPEL by St. Mark, in the *Abenaquis* Tongue. (Sine titulo.)—12mo. (E.)

AYMARA, with Spanish, (South America.)

El Evangeliode Jesu Christo Legun San Lucas, en *Aymará* y Español. Traducido de la Vulgata Latina, al Aymará por Don Vi cente Pazos; Hanki al Español por el P. Phelipe Scio de San Miguel. THE GOSPEL OF LUKE, translated from the Vulgate into the Aymaric and Spanish tongues.—12mo, London, 1829. (E.)

CHEROKEE.

THE GOSPEL by Matthew, the Acts of the Apostles, and other selections from the Holy Scriptures, with Hymns; translated into the *Cherokee* Language, by S. A. Worcester and E. Boudinot. American Board of Commissioners for Foreign Missions.—24mo, New Echota, 1832. (E.)

THE GOSPELS by Matthew and John, the Acts of the Apostles, the Epistles of John, and other selections from the Scriptures, with Hymns; translated into *Cherokee*. Mission Press.—32mo, Park Hill, 1840–3. Five copies. (E.)

CHIPPEWA.

Kekitchemanitomenahu, Gahbemahjeinnunk Jesus Christ Otoashke waween dummahgawin. THE NEW TESTAMENT in the *Chippewa* Language. Printed by Packard and Van Benthuysen.—12mo, Albany, 1833. (E.)

See also *Ojibwa*.

CHOCTAW.

Holisso Holitope, Chitoka ka Chisus im Anumpeshi Luk. Chani italuklo Kut Holissachi tokmako. Akasha Kut chahta im Arunpa isht holisso hoke.—12mo, Utica, 1831. (E.)

A Harmony of the Four Gospels in the *Choctaw* Language.

DAKOTA.

Wicoicage Wowopa qa odowan wakau Heberi iapi etauhan Kagapi pejihuta Wicaxta, psincinca, qa tamakoce, okagapi Kin hena eepi. THE BOOK OF GENESIS, and part of the BOOK OF PSALMS, in the *Dakota* Language; translated from the original Hebrew, by the Missionaries of the American Board of Commissioners of Foreign Missions and J. Renville, Sen. Printed for the Board.—12mo, Cincinnati, 1842. (E.)

THE BOOK OF GENESIS, part of the PSALMS, with the Gospels of LUKE and JOHN, in the *Dakota* Language. Vol. II. THE BOOK OF ACTS, the EPISTLES OF PAUL, and the REVELATION. First volume printed for the American Board of Commissioners of Foreign Missions; the second by the American Bible Society.—12mo, 1842. (E.)

DELAWARE.

THE EPISTLES OF ST. JOHN, in the *Delaware* Indian Language. Printed for the American Bible Society.—12mo, New York, 1818. (E.)

ESQUIMAUX, (North America.)

THE GOSPELS by St. Matthew, St. Mark, St. Luke, and St. John; translated into the Language of the *Esquimaux* Indians on the coast of Labrador, by the Missionaries of the "United Brethren," &c. Printed by the British and Foreign Bible Society.—12mo, London, 1813. (E.)

The Gospel by John is wanting in this copy.

Davidibib Assingdalo Tuksiaruktingit Nertordleruting-illo Lingerusertaggit. The Book of PSALMS, in the *Esquimaux* Language, as above.—12mo, London, 1830. (E.)

MASSACHUSETTS.

ELLIOT'S INDIAN BIBLE.—4to, Cambridge, 1635. (E.)

MOHAWK.

Neue Karighwiyoston Tsinihorighhotenne St. John. THE GOSPEL BY ST. JOHN, in the *Mohawk* Tongue. Printed for the British and Foreign Bible Society.—12mo, London, 1804. Four copies. (E.)

Ne Tsinchhoweyea—Neuda—Onh. Orighwa do Geaty. Roghyadon Royado Geaghty, Saint Luke. THE GOSPEL ACCORDING TO ST. LUKE, translated into the *Mohawk* Language, &c. Printed for the American Bible Society.—12mo, New York, 1827. (E.)

Two copies. The English text accompanies the Mohawk, in this version, on the right hand page.

Ne Raorihwadogenhti ne Shongwayaner Yesus Keristus Jenihorihoten ne Royatadogenhti Matthew, &c. THE GOSPEL ACCORDING TO ST. MATTHEW, translated into the *Mohawk* Language, &c. Printed by McElrath and Bangs for the Young Men's Auxiliary Methodist Bible Society.—12mo, New York, 1831. (E.)

The English text, in this version, is on the left hand page.

Ne Raorihwadogenhti ne Shongwayaner Yesus Keristus Jenihorihoten ne Royatadogenhti Luke, &c., &c. THE GOSPEL ACCORDING TO ST. LUKE, translated into the *Mohawk* Language, &c. Printed as above. —12mo, New York, 1833. (E.)

The English text is on the right hand page, and the translation on the left.

MOHEGAN.

THE MOHEGAN BIBLE.—4to, Cambridge, 1685. (E.)

OJIBWA.

Mesah oowh menwahjemoowin, Kahenahjemood owh St. Matthew. THE GOSPEL BY ST. MATTHEW, in the *Ojibwa* Language. Printed for the York (Canada) Auxiliary Bible Society.—8vo, York, (Canada,) 1831. (E.)

SENECA.

CHRIST'S SERMON ON THE MOUNT.—18mo, New York, 1829. (E.)

AMHARIC, (Old Ethiopic.)

Novum Testamentum Domini nostri et Servatoris Jesu Christi, sub auspiciis D. Asselini Rerum Gallicarum apud Ægyptios Procuratoris in Linguam Amharicam veitit Abu-Rumi Habessinus. Edidit Thomas Peel Platt. Printed for the British and Foreign Bible Society.—4to, London, 1829. (E.)

This is a very difficult dialect to write or learn.

ARABIC. (See also Coptic.)

The Holy Bible, containing the Old and New Testaments, in the *Arabic* Language. Printed by Sarah Hodgson.—4to, Newcastle upon Tyne, 1811. (H.)

A fine specimen of the Arabic Bible, from the Polyglott text, executed by J. D. Carlyle, Professor of Arabic in the University of Cambridge, under the patronage of the Bishop of Durham. For defraying the expense of the edition, the Society for Promoting Christian Knowledge contributed £500, and the British and Foreign Bible Society, £250.

Psalterium, a V. Scialac et G. Sionita, Arab. Lat.—4to, Rome, 1614. (H.)

The Holy Scriptures, in the *Arabic* Language.—8vo, London, 1820. (H.)

The New Testament, &c., in the *Arabic* Tongue.—8vo, Calcutta, 1816. Two copies. (H.)

Psalterium, or the Book of Psalms, in *Arabic*.—12mo, London, 1819. (H.)

The Book of Psalms, in the *Arabic* Language. Printed at the expense of the American Bible Society. Second edition.—12mo, Beyroot. Two copies. (H.)

ARMENIAN.

Biblia Sacra, or the Holy Bible, in the *Armenian* Language, (with Plates.)—4 vols. 8vo, Venice, 1805. (D.)

The Armenian is spoken between the Caspian and Black Seas.

Novum Testamentum, or the New Testament, in Ancient *Armenian*. Published by direction of the Russian Bible Society.—8vo, St. Petersburgh, 1814. Two copies. (D.)

Biblia Sacra, or the Holy Bible, in the *Armenian* Tongue. Printed by the Russian Bible Society.—4to, St. Petersburgh, 1817. (D.)

Biblia Sacra, or the Holy Bible, in the *Armenian* Language. Reprinted by order of the Calcutta Auxiliary Bible Society, at the Mission Press.—4to, Serampore, 1817. (D.)

Novum Testamentum, or the New Testament, in Ancient and Modern *Armenian*, arranged in parallel columns.—4to, Paris, 1828. (D.)

The Four Gospels, in Ancient *Armenian*.—18mo, Smyrna, 1837. Three copies. (D.)

Novum Testamentum; the New Testament, in Modern *Armenian*.—18mo, Smyrna, 1838. (D.)

Novum Testamentum; the New Testament, in Ancient *Armenian*. Printed at the expense of the American Bible Society.—18mo, Smyrna, 1838. Three copies; one in calf. (D.)

The Book of Psalms, in the *Armenian* Language.—18mo, Smyrna, 1838. (D.)

Novum Testamentum; the New Testament, in the *Armenian* Tongue (Baptist version.)—8vo, Calcutta, 1839. (D.)

The Book of Psalms, in the *Armenian* Language.—18mo, Smyrna, 1840. Five copies. (D.)

Novum Testamentum; the New Testament, in Modern *Armenian*.—12mo, Smyrna, 1842. Two copies. (D.)

The Apostolical Epistles and the Book of the Revelation, in Ancient *Armenian*, from the translation made in the fourth and fifth centuries.—18mo, Smyrna, 1843. Three copies. (D.)

The Book of Psalms, in the *Armenian* Language.—18mo, Smyrna, 1843. Five copies. (D.)

The Book of the Acts, the Apostolical Epistles, and the Book of the Revelation, in the *Armenian* Tongue.—18mo, Smyrna, 1843. (D.)

The Pentateuch, in Modern *Armenian*.—12mo, Smyrna, 1847. (D.)

Biblia Sacra, or the Holy Bible, &c., in Modern *Armenian*. Printed at the expense of the American Bible Society.—4to, Smyrna, 1853. (D.)

ARMENO-TURKISH.

Novum Testamentum; the New Testament, in *Armeno-Turkish*. Published by the Russian Bible Society.—12mo, St. Petersburgh, 1819. (D.)

NOVUM TESTAMENTUM, &c., in *Armeno-Turkish.*—8vo, Malta, 1831. (D.)

THE PENTATEUCH, in *Armeno-Turkish.*—12mo, Smyrna, 1840.—Ten copies; one unbound. (D.)

The Historical Books of the Old Testament, (Genesis to Esther inclusive,) in *Armeno-Turkish.*—12mo, Smyrna, 1841. Six copies; one gilt. (D.)

THE HAGIOGRAPHA of the Old Testament, (from the Book of Job to Malachi inclusive,) in *Armeno-Turkish.*—12mo, Smyrna, 1842. Five copies; one gilt. (D.)

NOVUM TESTAMENTUM, &c., in *Armeno-Turkish.*—12mo, Smyrna, 1843. Six copies; one gilt. (D.)

ASSAM, (India.)

THE HOLY BIBLE, containing the Old and New Testaments, translated from the originals into the *Assam* Language, by the Serampore Missionaries. Vol. V., containing the New Testament. Mission Press.—8vo, Serampore, 1820. (E.)

Two copies. The Assam dialect is spoken northeast of Bengal.

BENGALEE, (India.)

THE PENTATEUCH, in the *Bengalee* Language.—8vo, Serampore, 1819. (E.)

THE GOSPEL according to Matthew and John, in *English* and *Bengalee.* Printed at the Mission Press for the Calcutta Auxiliary Bible Society.—12mo, Calcutta, 1819. (E.)

THE GOSPEL according to Matthew and John, in *English* and *Bengalee.* Printed as above.—8vo, Calcutta, 1819. (E.)

THE PSALMS OF DAVID, translated into the *Bengalee* Language from the original Hebrew. Printed at the Baptist Mission Press for the Calcutta Auxiliary Bible Society.—8vo, Calcutta, 1826. (E.)

THE HOLY BIBLE, translated from the original Hebrew into the *Bengalee* Language, by the Serampore Missionaries. Vol. I., containing the Pentateuch and Historical Books.—8vo, Serampore, 1829. (E.)

THE FOUR GOSPELS, in *Bengalee.* Printed at the Baptist Mission Press for the Baptist Missionary Society.—8vo, Calcutta, 1831. (E.)

THE HOLY BIBLE, translated out of the original Tongues into the *Bengalee* Language, by the Serampore Missionaries.—8vo, Serampore, 1832. (E.)

THE FOUR GOSPELS, and the Acts of the Apostles, in *Bengalee.* Printed at the Baptist Mission Press for the Baptist Missionary Society.—8vo, Calcutta, 1837. (E.)

THE PSALMS of David, translated into the *Bengalee* Language from the original Hebrew. Printed at the Baptist Mission Press, &c. —12mo, Calcutta, 1838. (E.)

THE NEW TESTAMENT, &c., in the *Bengalee* Language, translated from the Greek by the Calcutta Baptist Missionaries, with native assistants. Printed as above for the American and Foreign Bible Society.—8vo, Calcutta, 1839. (E.)

THE BOOK OF GENESIS, and part of Exodus, in *Bengalee,* translated from the Hebrew as above. Printed for the Bible Translation Society, &c.—12mo, Calcutta, 1840. (E.)

THE GOSPEL according to St. John, in the *Bengalee* Language. No place or date. (E.)

THE BOOK of the Acts of the Apostles, in *Bengalee.* No place or date.—8vo. Pamphlet. (E.)

THE EPISTLE of Paul to the Romans, in *Bengalee.* No place or date.—8vo. Pamphlet. (E.)

The FIRST EPISTLE of Paul to the Corinthians, in *Bengalee.* No place or date.—8vo. Pamphlet. (E.)

BOHEMIAN.

BIBLJ SWATA, or the Holy Bible, in the *Bohemian* Language.—8vo, Berlin, 1813. (D.)

BIBLJ SWATA, or the Holy Bible, in the *Bohemian* Language.—8vo, Ryseku, 1848. (D.)

BIKANEER. (See Vikaneera.)

BULGARIAN.

Novyi z aviat Gospode nashego Jecoosa Christa Cega, nóva Prevedennoi ô Slavenskago na Bólgarskii iazyk B' Smyrna. THE NEW TESTAMENT of our Lord Jesus Christ. A new translation from the Slavonic into *Bulgarian.*—8vo, Smyrna, 1840. (E.)

BULLOM, (African.)

Booh Hoa Matthew, or the Gospel according to St. Matthew, in *Bullom* and *English*.—12mo, London, 1816. (E.)

BURMAN.

The New Testament, in the *Burman* Language. First edition.—8vo, Maulmein, 1832. (E.)

The Old Testament, in the *Burman* Language. Vol. II., from 1 Samuel to Job inclusive.—8vo, Maulmein, 1834. (E.)

CALMUC, (Tartar.)

The Gospel according to St. Matthew, translated into the *Calmuc* dialect.—4to, St. Petersburgh, 1815. Two copies. (E.)

CARELIAN. (See Slavonic.)

CARSHUN.

The New Testament, translated into *Carshun* and *Syriac*, arranged in parallel columns.—4to, Paris, 1824. (E.)

The Carshun is the Arabic language in Syriac characters.

The New Testament, in the *Carshun* Language.—4to, Paris, 1827. (E.)

CHINESE.

The Books of the Old Testament, (Historical,) from Genesis to Esther inclusive, with the entire New Testament, in the *Chinese* Language.—4 vols. 8vo, Serampore, 1815-22. Pamphlets. (D.)

Printed with metallic moveable characters.

The Sacred Books of the Old Testament, translated into the *Chinese* Language. In five parts.—5 vols. 8vo, Serampore, 1818-21. Pamphlets. (D.)

Printed with metallic moveable characters.

The Holy Scriptures of the Old and New Testaments, translated into the *Chinese* Language, by Morrison and Milne. Issued from the Anglo-Chinese College (London Missionary Society).—21 vols. 18mo, Canton, 1823. Two copies; one in a box. (D.)

The New Testament, translated into the *Chinese* Language, by Messrs. Medhurst and Gutzlaff.—3 vols. 8vo, Singapore, 1836. Pamphlets. (D.)

There are duplicate copies of Mark and John.

The Pentateuch, in the *Chinese* Language. From the British and Foreign Bible Society.—4to. (D.)

The New Testament, in *Chinese*, in eight parts.—8 vols. 12mo, Canton, 1814. Three sets, in cases. (D.)

The New Testament, in *Chinese*. Stereotyped version, by Medhurst.—3 vols. 8vo. Two copies. (D.)

The Sacred Books of the Old Testament, translated into the *Chinese* Language. A new Version, by Medhurst.—4 vols. 8vo. (D.)

Two other Chinese books not described.—2 vols. 12mo. (D.)

The New Testament, &c., translated into the *Chinese* Language by the Committee of Delegates from the Protestant Missionaries in China for that purpose, and printed under their supervision for the British and Foreign Bible Society. The blanks left in the text by them for the words representing Theos and Pneuma, being filled by the Shanghae Corresponding Committee of the British and Foreign Bible Society. London Missionary Society Press.—8vo, Shanghae, 1852. Pamphlet. (D.)

The Gospel according to St. Luke, translated by the Presbyterian Mission and the Church Missionary brethren at Ningpo, into the *Ningpo* (China) colloquial language. Printed at the Presbyterian Mission Press.—8vo, Ningpo, 1852. (D.)

Printed in Roman letters. In general, the Continental sound of the vowels is used, as also the Italian *c;* ô as *o* in Lord; ʻ for aspirates, &c. The whole edition of 700 copies is said to have cost about $55.

The Gospel according to St. Matthew, translated by the Rev. W. P. Martin of the Presbyterian Mission, and the Rev. W. A. Russell of the Church Missionary Society, into the colloquial dialect of *Ningpo* (China).—8vo, Ningpo, 1853. (D.)

Printed in Roman letters, which were cut on blocks according to impressions stamped on paper by horn type.

The Gospel according to St. John, translated into the *Ningpo* (China) colloquial language by the Rev. W. P. Martin of the Presbyterian Board, U. S. A., and Rev. W. A. Russell of the Church Missionary Society, England.—8vo, Ningpo, 1853. (D.)

Printed in Roman letters, cut on Chinese blocks, at the cost of *one eighth* of a cent for each sound, as *to*, *siang*, *zông*, &c. The cost of cutting the whole volume was about $34. The cost of printing an edition of 500 copies was about $60; and every additional one hundred copies, about $4.

THE NEW TESTAMENT, in Chinese characters. Published by the London Missionary Society.—8vo, Hong Kong, 1854. (D.)

THE NEW TESTAMENT, in Chinese characters. Published by the London Missionary Society.—2 vols. 8vo, Canton, 1854. (D.)

Printed on Chinese blocks, and furnished at 14 cents per Testament.

CHOCTAW. (See American Indian.)

CINGALESE or SINGHALESE (Ceylon).

THE NEW TESTAMENT, &c., translated into the *Cingalese* Language under the direction of the Colombo Auxiliary Bible Society, and the patronage of His Excellency Sir Robert Brownrigg, Governor of Ceylon.—4to, Colombo, 1817. (E.)

COPTIC.

The Book of Psalms, translated into *Coptic* and *Arabic*.—4to, London, 1826. (H.)

The Coptic is a dialect of Ethiopia.

The Four Gospels, in *Coptic* and *Arabic*.—4to, London, 1829. (H.)

DANISH.

BIBLIA SACRA; the Holy Bible, in the *Danish* Language, with a Register, &c. Illustrated with Plates.—Fol., Copenhagen, 1633. (D.)

BIBLIA, det er den gandste Hellige Scriftes; the Holy Scriptures, in the *Danish* Language.—8vo, Copenhagen, 1799. (D.)

THE NEW TESTAMENT, in the *Danish* Language.—12mo, London, 1812. (E.)

Det Nye Testamente oversat fra Grundsproget; The New Testament, in *Danish*, from the original Language. Printed for the British and Foreign Bible Society. Fourteenth edition.—8vo, London, 1814. (E.)

Biblia Sacra; the Holy Scriptures, in the *Danish* Language. (Sextende Oplag.)—8vo, Copenhagen, 1819. (D.)

Biblia Sacra; the Holy Bible, translated into the *Danish* Language.—Roy. 8vo, London, 1829. (D.)

DORPATIAN. (See Esthonian.)

DUTCH.

Biblia Sacra, &c. Old Holland version.—Fol., Amsterdam, 1603. (O.)

This copy is imperfect.

Biblia; or, Des Ouden en Des Nieuwen Testaments, &c., with the Apocrypha.—12mo, Dort, 1614. (D.)

Imperfect. Printed in German characters. Psalms set to music.

Biblia, &c., as above, in German characters.—12mo, Amsterdam, 1624. (D.)

Biblia Sacra; the Holy Bible, &c.—Fol., Graven Hage, 1642. (M.)

This copy is imperfect. The title page of the Old Testament is wanting, and that of the New Testament has no date. The date above is from a memorandum in writing on a blank leaf of the volume.

Biblia, &c. In Roman characters.—18mo, Amsterdam, 1662. (D.)

Biblia, &c.—Fol., Leyden, 1663. (M.)

Biblia, &c., with Maps.—Fol., Dort and Amsterdam, 1690. Two copies. (M.)

Nieuwe Testament, &c.—18mo, Amsterdam, 1693. (D.)

This copy is imperfect.

Biblia, &c. Illustrated.—Fol., Dort and Amsterdam, 1702. (M.)

Biblia, &c.—4to, Dort and Amsterdam, 1710. (O.)

Het Nieuwe Testament, oste alle Boecken des Nieuwen Verbonts onses Heeren Jesu Christi.—18mo, Amsterdam, 1710. (D.)

In German characters, with a Liturgy, and Psalms set to music.

Biblia, dat is De gantsche H. Schrift, &c. Illustrated with Plates.—Fol., Amsterdam, 1718. Three copies. (N and O.)

Biblia, des Ouden en des Nieuwen Testaments, &c., with Annotations. Illustrated.—Fol., Dort and Amsterdam, 1719. (N.)

Biblia, &c., as above. In German characters.—8vo, Dort, 1720. (D.)

Biblia, &c.—4to, Amsterdam, 1723. (O.)

Biblia, &c. In German characters, with Liturgy.—12mo, Dort, 1723. (D.)

Het Nieuwe Testament, &c. In German characters.—18mo, Amsterdam, 1726. (D.)

Biblia, &c. Illustrated.—Fol., Dort, 1729. (M.)

Biblia, &c., with Annotations, Plates, Maps, &c.—Fol., Dort, 1730. Two copies. (M.)

Het Nieuwe Testament, with Liturgy and Psalms.—18mo, Amsterdam, 1734. Imperfect. (D.)

Biblia, &c. Illustrated.—Fol., Dort, 1736. Copy imperfect. (O.)

Biblia, &c., with Catechism, Liturgy, and Psalms set to music.—4to, Amsterdam, 1738. (O.)

Het Nieuwe Testament, with Liturgy, &c.—18mo, Amsterdam, 1737. (D.)

Biblia, dat is De gantsche H. Schrifture, &c. In German characters.—18mo, Dort, 1740. (D.)

This was once an elegant copy, in gilt binding.

Biblia, &c. In German characters.—8vo, Amsterdam, 1740. (D.)

Biblia, des Ouden en des Nieuwen Testaments, &c. Illustrated with Maps and Plates.—Fol., Dort, 1741. Four copies. (N.)

Biblia, &c., as above, with the Apocrypha.—Fol., Dort, 1744. Two copies. (O.)

Biblia, &c.—4to, Amsterdam, 1745. (O.)

Het Nieuwe Testament, &c. In German characters.—18mo, Dort, 1746. (D.)

Het Nieuwe Testament, &c.—18mo, Amsterdam, 1746. (D.)

De Bybel, &c. Embellished with Maps.—Fol., Gorinchem, 1748. (M.)

Biblia, &c. In German characters.—18mo, Dort, 1750. (D.)

Biblia, &c., with Catechism, and Psalms set to music.—4to, Amsterdam, 1754. (O.)

Het Nieuwe Testament, &c.—18mo, Amsterdam, 1757. (D.)

Biblia, dat is De gantsche H. Schrift, &c.—12mo, Amsterdam, 1757-8. (D.)

Het Nieuwe Testament, &c., with Liturgy. In German characters.—18mo, Amsterdam, 1759. (D.)

Biblia, dat is De gantsche H. Schrift, &c. In German characters.—4to, Amsterdam, 1761. (D.)

Biblia, &c.—8vo, Amsterdam, 1766. (D.)

Het Nieuwe Testament, &c.—18mo, Amsterdam, 1770. (D.)

Het Nieuwe Testament, &c. No date.—18mo. (D.)

Biblia, de gantsche H. Schrift, &c. In German characters.—18mo, Amsterdam, 1774. (D.)

Biblia, &c., with Liturgy, plates, &c. In German characters.—2 vols. 12mo, Haarlem, 1776-78. (D.)

Het Nieuwe Testament. In German characters.—18mo, Dort, 1778. (D.)

Der Psalmen.—12mo, Dort, 1778. (D.)

Nieuwe Testament.—18mo, Amsterdam, 1778. (D.)

Biblia, or des Ouden en des Nieuwen Testaments.—8vo, London, 1812. Two copies. (D.)

Het Nieuwe Testament. In Roman characters.—12mo, Bermondsey, 1814. (D.)

Die Bibel, oder die ganze Heilige Schrift des Alten und Neuen Testaments, &c.—8vo, Hamburgh, 1821. (D.)

De Bybel, dat is des Ouden en Nieuwen Testaments. In Roman characters.—8vo, London, 1846. (D.)

Het Nieuwe Testament, of alle de Boeken des Nieuwen Verbonds van onzen Heer Jezus Christus, &c.—8vo, Dort, 1846. (D.)

ESQUIMAUX. (See American Indian.)

ESTHONIAN or DORPATIAN.

Meije Isanda Jesusse Kristusse Uus Testament, ehk ue Seäd usse Ramat. The New Testament, &c., in the *Revalian Esthonian* Dialect.—8vo, Tallinas, 1790. (E.)

Another copy of the same.—8vo, Tallinas, 1816. (E.)

Meije Isanda Jesusse Kristusse Wastne Testament. The New Testament of our Lord Jesus Christ, in *Dorpatian Esthonian.*—8vo, Mitau, 1815. (E.)

Two copies. This dialect is spoken east of the Baltic Sea.

Meie Isanda Jesusse Kristusse Uus Testament, ehk ue Seäd usse Ramat, ja Kunuinga Taweti Lanlo Ramat. The New Testament of our Lord Jesus Christ, and King David's Psalms, in the *Esthonian* Language. Printed for the American Bible Society.—8vo, Helsingfors, 1852. (E.)

ETHIOPIC.

Psalterium Davidis Aethiopice. Printed for the British and Foreign Bible Society.—8vo, London, 1815. (H.)

FINNISH, (North of Europe.)

Uusi Testamenti. The New Testament, in the *Finnish* Language.—8vo, Turusa, 1775. (E.)

Spoken east of St. Petersburgh, on the Baltic.

Uusi Testamenti. The New Testament, in the *Finnish* Language. Published by the Finnish Bible Society.—8vo, Turusa, 1815. (E.)

BIBLIA, eli Pyha Raamattu Wanha ia Uusi Testamenti. THE BIBLE, or Books of the Old and New Testaments. Published by the Finnish Bible Society.—8vo, St. Petersburgh, 1817. (E.)

Uusi Testamenti. THE NEW TESTAMENT, &c. Published by the Finnish Bible Society.—8vo, St. Petersburgh, 1822. (E.)

FRENCH.

LA SAINCTE BIBLE, au Francoys translata Selon la pure et entiere traduction de St. Hierome, &c. En Auves par Martin Lunpereur, &c.—Fol., 1534. (F.)

This is the third edition of the French Bible, printed in beautiful Gothic letter, and has numerous curious woodcuts, various readings explanatory of the text, and marginal notes. The title page to the Old Testament is wanting, and much of the preliminary matter; also, the Apocalypse, except the first eight chapters. This edition is in the Index of prohibited books.

LA SAINTE BIBLE, &c.—Fol., Geneva, 1565. (F.)

Imperfect. It has Beza's Epistle, Calvin's Preface, and the usual preliminary matter, marginal readings, notes, &c. It is therefore a Protestant version. All the title pages are wanting; but the following memorandum is written on the cover: "This is the earliest edition of the French Bible, commonly called Calvin's Bible, being printed under his direction by the celebrated Etienne, A.D. 1565. The translation commenced in 1535."

LA SAINCTE BIBLE, en Francois avec les argumens sur chacun livre declarans sommairement tout ce que y est contenu, par Barthelemi Honorati.—8vo, Lyons, 1582. (F.)

A Catholic version. The figures before each verse are inserted in the text. It has over three hundred wood engravings. It has no title page to the New Testament. A table of Epistles and Gospels to be read in the Churches is appended.

LA BIBLE, qui est toute la Saincte Escriture du vieil et Noover Testament. Autrement, l'Ancienne et la Nouvelle Alliance. Le tout reue et conferé sur les textes Hebrieux et Grecs, &c.—12mo, Sedan, 1633. (F.)

A Protestant version, printed in a very small but clear letter.

LA BIBLE, qui est toute la Saincte Escriture du vieil et du Nouveau Testament; autrement l'Ancienne et la Nouvelle Alliance. Le tout reue a conferé sur les textes Hebrieux et Grecs, par les Pasteurs et Professeurs de l'Eglise de Geneve, &c., &c. Imprime pour Jacques Chouët.—Fol., Geneva, 1644. (F.)

A Protestant version, with Beza's Epistle, Calvin's Preface, tables of contents, arguments, summaries, marginal notes, maps, index, &c. It has the Psalms of David in metre, set to music, Prayers, Catechism and Confession of Faith, with a list of quotations from the Old Testament into the New.

LA SAINTE BIBLE, interprete par Jean Diodati. Imprime par Pierre Chovët.—Fol., Geneva, 1644. (F.)

Two copies. This is the first edition of the Protestant version of Diodati, considered by Father Simon as a paraphrase rather than a translation. It has notes, summaries, and parallel passages.

LA SAINTE BIBLE, qui contient le Vieux et le Nouveau Testament. Edition nouvelle, faite sur la version de Geneve, reveue et corrigee; enrichee, outre les anciennes notes, de toutes celles de la Bible Flamande, de la plus-part de celles de M. Diodati, et beaucoup d'autres, &c., &c., par les soins de S. et H. Des Marets.—2 vols. fol., Amsterdam, 1669. (F.)

Two copies, both on large paper. This is a Protestant edition, and the most magnificent French Bible ever printed. It was based on the edition of 1652 by P. De Hayes, the most correct then extant. It has notes from the German Bible and the Flamand Bible of 1637, with those of Diodati. The Apocrypha is placed after the New Testament. It has maps of the land of Canaan, the travels of the Apostles, the city of Jerusalem (from Walton's Polyglott), &c., &c.

LE NOUVEAU TESTAMENT de nostre Seigneur Jesus Christ, traduit en François, selon edition Vulgate, avec les differences du Grec. Nouvelle et derniere edition, revue et corrigee tres-exactment, chez Gaspard Miglot, &c.—12mo, Mons, 1673. (F.)

A Catholic edition.

LE NOUVEAU TESTAMENT, c'est a dire la Nouvelle Alliance de nostre Seigneur Jesus Christ.—16mo, 1676. (F.)

This is a Protestant edition, without date, except that of the Psalms of David in Metre at the end of the work, which is 1676.

LE NOUVEAU TESTAMENT de notre Seigneur Jesus Christ, traduit selon l'ancienne edition Latine, corrigee par le commandement du Pape Sixte V., par D. Aurelote.—8vo, Paris, 1677. (F.)

A Catholic edition.

LA SAINTE BIBLE, qui contient l'Ancien et le Nouveau Testament, c'est à dire l'Ancienne et la Nouvelle Alliance, &c.—4to, Geneva, 1690. (F.)

A Protestant translation, with an Epistle to the Reader and Calvin's Preface.

LES PSEAUMES DE DAVID, Mis en rime Francoise, par Clement Marot et Theodore de Beze.—12mo, Amsterdam, 1693. (F.)

LE NOUVEAU TESTAMENT de notre Seigneur Jesus Christ; Explique par des notes conte et Caire, sur le version ordinaire, des Eglises Reformees, avec une Preface generale touchant la verite de la religion chrétienne; et diverses autres prefaces particulieres sur chacun des Livres du Nouveau Testament, par David Martin.—4to, Utrecht, 1696. (F.)

One of the best Protestant versions.

LA SAINTE BIBLE, qui contient le Vieux et le Nouveau Testament, &c. Avec le Indices, et remarques necessaires pour l'instruction du Lecteur, et les Psaumes des David, &c.—4to, Amsterdam, 1700. (F.)

This is Calvin's translation, revised by the pastors of Geneva. It is generally called the Geneva Bible. It has the Epistle of Beza and the Preface of Calvin. The Apocrypha is at the end of the volume.

LA SAINTE BIBLE, qui contient le Vieaux et le Nouveau Testament, &c. Le tout revue et conferé sur le textes Hebreux et Grecs, par les pasteurs et les professeurs de l'Eglise de Geneve, &c.—Fol., Amsterdam, 1702. (F.)

A Protestant version, similar to the foregoing.

LA SAINTE BIBLE, &c., expliques par des notes de Theologie et de Critique sur la version ordinaire des Eglises Reformees, revue sur les Originaux, et retouchee dans la langage, &c., par David Martin, Pasteur de l'Eglise Wallone d'Utrecht. Henry Desbordes, Pierre Mortier, et Pierre Brunel.—2 vols. fol., Amsterdam, 1707. (F.)

This is the first edition of this celebrated Protestant version. It is the Geneva version, revised and corrected so materially as frequently to be considered a new translation. With the usual notes, prefaces, &c., it has some general considerations respecting the Christian religion, which have been printed separately.

LA SAINTE BIBLE, qui contient l'Ancien et le Nouveau Testament.—12mo, Amsterdam, 1710. (F.)

Two copies; one imperfect. Without summaries, marginal notes, or parallel passages. Has the Psalms in Metre, Articles of Faith, Catechism, &c., of the Reformed Churches.

LA SAINTE BIBLE, traduit sur les textes originaux, avec les differences de la Vulgate. Le Gros's version.—12mo, Cologne, 1739. (F.)

This is a Catholic version; partly an original translation, though generally conformed to the Vulgate. The passages in which it differs are inclosed in brackets; and where the translation has been made from the Syriac, Hebrew, Samaritan, or Septuagint, they are marked by particular Italics.

LA SAINTE BIBLE, &c., avec le argumens et les reflexions sur les chaptres de l'Ecriture Sainte et des notes, par J. F. Ostervald.—Fol., Neufchatel, 1772. (F.)

A Protestant version, and is a revision of the Genevan. The argument and reflections are esteemed valuable. This is considered the best edition of Ostervald's Bible. It has the Apocrypha.

LE NOUVEAUX TESTAMENT en Latin et en Francais, traduit par Sacy. Edition ornee de Figures gravees sur les dessins de Moreau le jeune.—4 vols. 8vo, Paris, 1793. (F.)

These four volumes, which contain the Gospels, are the only portion of this fine edition of De Sacy's version in the Library.

LE NOUVEAU TESTAMFNT de notre Seigneur Jesus Christ. Imprime sur l'edition de Paris, de l'Annee 1805. Printed for the British and Foreign Bible Society.—12mo, London, 1807. (F.)

Le Nouveau Testament de notre Seigneur Jesus Christ, en Français, sur la Vulgate. Traduction de L. M. De Sacy. Revue sur les Meilleures Editions. De l'imprimerie de J. T. Buckingham.—2 vols. in 1, 8vo, Boston, 1810.

This edition is printed in paragraphs, the place of the verses being denoted by figures in the margin.

La Sainte Bible, &c., par les pasteurs et professeurs de l'Eglise de Geneve. Edition Stereotype, revue et corrigee. Printed for the British and Foreign Bible Society.—12mo, London, 1811. (F.)

Le Nouveau Testament de notre Seigneur Jesus Christ. D'apres la traduction d'Ostervald. Edition Stereotype.—8vo, Paris, 1813. (F.)

La Sainte Bible, le Vieux et le Nouveaux Testament, &c.—12mo, New York, 1815. (F.)

Le Nouveau Testament, selon la Vulgate, reimprime sur la traduction Françaisе de le M. De Sacy. Russian Bible Society.—8vo, St. Petersburgh, 1815. (F.)

Le Nouveau Testament, &c., traduit sur la Vulgate par le M. De Sacy.—12mo, Paris, 1817. (F.)

Le Nouveau Testament, &c. French and English. Printed for the British and Foreign Bible Society.—8vo, London, 1817. (F.)

La Sainte Bible, &c., traduite sur la Vulgate par le M. De Saci. Russian Bible Society.—8vo, St. Petersburgh, 1817. (F.)

La Sainte Bible, &c., revue sur les originaux et retouchee dans le langage, par David Martin. Paris Protestant Bible Society.—2 vols. 8vo, Toulouse, 1819. Two copies. (F.)

La Sainte Bible, &c., avec paralleles et des sommaires, par D. Martin; revue et corrigee, par Pierre Roques.—4to, Montauban, 1819. (F.)

La Sainte Bible, &c., par David Martin.—8vo, Paris, 1820. (F.)

This edition has the parallel passages.

Le Nouveau Testament de notre Seigneur Jesus Christ, traduction de D. Martin, avec paralleles.—16mo, Paris, 1820. (F.)

Le Nouveau Testament de notre Seigneur Jesus Christ, traduit sur la Vulgate par le M. De Sacy.—12mo, Paris, 1820. Two copies. (F.)

La Sainte Bible, &c.—8vo, Basle, 1821. (F.)

This is Ostervald's version, though his name is not on the title page.

La Sainte Bible, contenant l'Ancien et le Nouveau Testament, traduite sur la Vulgate, par le M. De Sacy.—8vo, Paris, 1821. (F.)

La Sainte Bible, ou l'Ancien et le Nouveau Testament. D'apres la version par J. F. Ostervald. Paris Protestant Bible Society.—8vo, Paris, 1824. Two copies. (F.)

Le Nouveau Testament, &c., traduit sur la Vulgate, par le M. De Sacy.—8vo, Paris, 1824. (F.)

Le Nouveaux Testament, sur l'edition de Paris de l'An. 1805. Printed by the American Bible Society.—12mo, New York, 1826. (F.)

Le Nouveau Testament, &c. D'apres la version revue par J. F. Ostervald.—12mo, Paris, 1826. (F.)

Le Nouveaux Testament, &c., par David Martin. Edicion Stereotype.—8vo, Montbeliard, 1826. (F.)

Le Nouveaux Testament, &c., par David Martin.—24mo, Paris, 1826. (F.)

Le Nouveaux Testament, &c., par David Martin. Nouvelle edition. De l'Imprimerie Navarre, 1819.—8vo, Toulouse, 1826. (F.)

Le Nouveaux Testament, &c. Revue par D. Martin.—12mo, Paris, 1827. (F.)

La Sainte Bible, qui contient le Vieux et le Nouveau Testament, par David Martin.—12mo, Paris, 1827. (F.)

La Sainte Bible, qui contient le Vieux et le Nouveau Testament. Revue sur les originaux, par David Martin.—8vo, Paris, 1827. (F.)

Li sent Evangele de notre Seigneur Gesu Christ, counfourma Sént Luc et Sént Giann: rendie en Lengua Valdesa Les Saints Evangiles, &c., selon St. Luc et St. Jean. Traduit en langue Vaudoise, par Pierre Bert.—8vo, London, 1830. (F.)

French and *Vaudois* Gospels of Luke and John.

Sainte Bible, &c., Imprimee sur l'edition de Paris de l'annee 1805. Edition Stereotype. Revue et corrigee avec soin d'apres les textes Hebreu et Grec. Printed for the British and Foreign Bible Society.—12mo, London, 1831. (F.)

La Bible, traduction Nouvelle, avec l'Hebreu en regard, accompagne des points-voyelles et des accens toniques, avec des notes philologiques, geographiques, et litteraires, et les principales variantes de la version des Septante et du text Samaritain, par T. Caheu, Directeur de l'Ecole Israelite de Paris.—5 vols. 8vo, Paris, 1831. (F.)

These five volumes contain the Pentateuch. The Hebrew text is on the right-hand page, and the French translation on the left.

LE NOUVEAU TESTAMENT de notre Seigneur Jesus Christ, d'apres la version revue par J. F. Ostervald.—12mo, 1840. (F.)

LE NOUVEAU TESTAMENT. De Sacy. Printed by the American Bible Society.—32mo, New York, 1843. Two copies. (F.)

LE NOUVEAU TESTAMENT, revue sur les originaux, par David Martin. Printed by the American Bible Society.—12mo, New York, 1844. Two copies. (F.)

LA SAINTE BIBLE, le Vieux et le Nouveau Testament, par D. Martin. Printed by the American Bible Society.—12mo, New York, 1846. (F.)

LA SAINTE BIBLE, &c.—8vo. (F.)

A Protestant version; but so defective that the date cannot be ascertained. It contains the French and English New Testament. The French is on the left-hand page, the English on the right.

GAELIC.

Leabhraichean an T—Seann Tiomnaidh. THE HOLY BIBLE, in the *Gaelic* Language.—12mo, Edinburgh, 1807. (E.)

Spoken in the Highlands of Scotland.

Tiomnaidh Nuadh ar Tighearna agus ar Slanuighir Josa Criosd. THE HOLY BIBLE, containing the Old and New Testaments, in the *Gaelic* Language. Printed for the British and Foreign Bible Society.—12mo, London, 1807. (E.)

This copy has the same title page to both the Old and New Testaments, with the difference of only an additional letter. The New Testament is imprinted at Chelsea.

Tiomnaidh Nuadh ar Tighearna agus ar Slanuighir Josa Criosd. THE NEW TESTAMENT, &c., in the *Gaelic* Tongue.—12mo, Edinburgh, 1813. (E.)

See, also, under *Manks*.

GEORGIAN.

THE NEW TESTAMENT, in the *Georgian* Language (*ecclesiastical* character, used between the Caspian and Black Seas).—4to, Moscow, 1816. (E.)

THE NEW TESTAMENT, in the *Georgian* Language (civil character).—4to, St. Petersburgh, 1818. (E.)

The civil character is the vulgar idiom, used among the people and in civil affairs; the ecclesiastical is known almost exclusively by the clergy and the learned, and confined to sacred literature. The civil is said to be a corruption of the ecclesiastical, holding a similar relation to it, as the Italian to the Latin. Not only the dialects, but the alphabets also, are different. Previous to the invention of the Armenian letters, the Georgians used the Greek ritual and language in both civil and ecclesiastical affairs. Since then the Georgian alphabet has been formed from the Armenian. The Georgian Psalms, prophetical books, and New Testament were printed at Tiffis at the commencement of the 18th century, and the entire Bible at Moscow in 1743. The Moscow Bible Society have printed two editions of the New Testament from this Bible; one in 1816, of 5000 copies, in the church character; the other of 2000, in 1818, in the civil character; both in quarto. [Henderson's Bible Researches. See Bib. Sussexiana, vol. ii., p. 83, 84.]

GERMAN.

Biblia Helvetica, or Die gantze Bibel, with illustrated title page and numerous plates.—Fol., Zurich, 1531. (E.)

This is one of the earliest editions of the German Bible.

Biblia, &c.—Fol., Frankfort on the Mayne, 1565. (F.)

This is an imperfect copy of this edition, originally containing all the books of the Old Testament, except the prophetical. It is printed in Black letter, and has numerous plates, maps, &c.

Biblia, &c.—12mo, Amsterdam, 1734. (F.)

Biblia, &c.—18mo, Amsterdam. (F.)

The title page is wanting, and it is without date.

Biblia, &c.—4to, Philadelphia. (F.)

Biblia; dat ist Die gantze Heilige Schrift. Illustrated with plates.—4to, Tubingen, 1745. (F.)

Die Bibel; with a Liturgy and the Augsburg Confession. —12mo, Stutgardt, 1756. (F.)

Biblia; dat is Die gantze Heilige Schrift; with plates.— 8vo, Tubingen, 1764. (F.)

Biblia, &c.—Fol., Nuremberg, 1765. (E.)

Two copies. This edition is embellished with portraits of the German princes, and of Luther and his family, and has the Augsburg Confession.

Biblia, &c.—4to, Germantown, 1776. (F.)

This is the third edition of the first Bible printed in America.

DIE BIBEL, &c.—12mo, Halle, 1794. (F.)

HEILIGE BUCHER DES NEUEN TESTAMENT.—12mo, Ratisbon, 1809. (F.)

DAS NEUE TESTAMENT.—24mo, London, 1812. (F.)

DAS NEUEN TESTAMENTES.—12mo, Ratisbon, 1812. (F.)

A Catholic version.

DIE GANTZE HEILIGE SCHRIFT.—8vo, London, 1813. (F.)

Two copies. A Lutheran version.

DIE BIBEL des Alten und Neuen Testaments, &c.—12mo, London, 1814. Two copies. (F.)

DAS NEUE TESTAMENT.—8vo, Munich, 1815. (F.)

This is Gosner's version.

DAS NEUE TESTAMENT.—32mo, Tubingen, 1815. (F.)

DIE BIBEL, &c.—8vo, Stutgardt, 1815. (F.)

DIE BIBEL, &c.—8vo, Stutgardt, 1815. (F.)

A duplicate of the preceding.

DAS NEUE TESTAMENT.—8vo, Basil, 1816. (F.)

DAS NEUE TESTAMENT.—18mo, Sulzbach, 1816. (F.)

This version is by Leander Van Ess.

DAS NEUE TESTAMENT.—8vo, Munich, 1816. (F.)

Gosner's Catholic version.

DIE BIBEL, &c.—Fol., Zurich, 1817. (F.)

DIE BIBEL, &c.—12mo, Breslau, 1817. (F.)

DAS NEUE TESTAMENT.—12mo, St. Petersburgh, 1817. (F.)

This is a Catholic version.

DIE BIBEL des Alten und Neuen Testaments, &c.—2 vols. 8vo, Zurich, 1817. (F.)

DIE BIBEL, dat ist alle Bucher der ganzen Heiligen Schrift des Alten und Neuen Testaments, &c.—Fol., Zurich, 1817. (E.)

DIE BIBEL, &c.—12mo, Frankfort (Mayn), 1818. (F.)

DAS NEUE TESTAMENT.—8vo, Hamburg, 1818. (F.)

Die Bibel, &c.—8vo, Basil, 1819. (F.)

Die Bibel, &c.—8vo, Strasburgh, 1819. (F.)

Die Bibel, &c.—12mo, Schleswig, 1819. (F.)

Das Neue Testament.—12mo, Germantown, 1819. (F.)

Die Bibel, &c.—8vo, Sleswick, 1819. (F.)

Das Neue Testament.—8vo, Sleswick, 1819. (F.)

Das Neue Testament.—8vo, Hamburgh, 1820. (F.)

Die Bibel, &c.—8vo, Basil, 1820. (F.)

Die Bibel, des Alten und Neuen Testaments.—8vo, Hamburgh, 1821. (F.)

Die Bible, &c.—4to, Basil, 1821. (E.)

Die Bibel, &c.—12mo, Hamburgh, 1821. (F.)

Die Bibel, &c.—12mo, Bremen, 1822. (F.)

Das Neue Testament.—12mo, Germantown, 1822. (F.)

Das Neue Testament.—12mo, Bremen, 1822. (F.)

Die Bible, &c.—12mo, Hamburgh, 1824. (F.)

Die Bibel, &c.—8vo, Hamburgh, 1824. (F.)

Das Neue Testament.—12mo, Leipsic, 1825. (F.)

This is Gosner's version.

Das Neue Testament.—12mo, Paris, 1826. (F.)

Das Neue Testament.—24mo, London, 1827. (F.)

Die Bibel, &c.—8vo, London, 1827. (F.)

Die Bibel, &c.—8vo, Strasburgh, 1828. (F.)

Das Neue Testament.—12mo, Philadelphia, 1828. (F.)

Die Bibel, &c.—8vo, Basil, 1828. (F.)

Das Neue Testament.—12mo, Philadelphia, 1830. (F.)

Die Bibel; oder Die ganze Heilige Schrift des Alten und Neuen Testaments.—8vo, Philadelphia, 1830. (F.)

Die Bible, &c.—12mo, Philadelphia, 1834. (F.)

Das Neue Testament. Published by the American Bible Society.—8vo, New York, 1835. (F.)

Das Neue Testament.—24mo, Lintz (Austria), 1842. (F.)

Das Neue Testament. Printed at the expense of the American Bible Society.—24mo, Lintz, 1842. (F.)

Die Bibel, &c.—8vo, Halle, 1843. (F.)

Das Neue Testament.—24mo, Elberfeldt, 1849. (F.)

Das Neue Testament.—32mo, Elberfeldt, 1849. (F.)

Das Neue Testament und Psalmen.—12mo, Cologne, 1850. (F.)

Das Neue Testament.—12mo, Cologne, 1850. (F.)

Die Bibel; oder Die ganze Heilige Schrift des Alten und Neuen Testaments.—8vo, Leipsic, 1852. (F.)

This translation is after that of Luther, and contains his portrait.

GIPSEY.

Embeo e Majaro Lucas. Brotoboro randado andre la chipe Griega, acana chibado andre o Romano o' chipe es Zincales de Sese.

El Evangelio segun S. Lucas, traducido al Romani, e dialecto de los Gitanos de Espana.

The Gospel of St. Luke, in the *Gipsey* Language.—Sine loco. 12mo, 1837. (F.)

GOOZARATTEE, (India.)

The Holy Bible, containing the Old and New Testaments, translated from the Originals into the *Goozarattee* Language by the Serampore Missionaries. Vol. V., containing the New Testament. Printed at the Mission Press.—8vo, Serampore, 1820. (E.)

This language is spoken northwest of the peninsula of Hindostan.

GREBO, (African.)

The Gospel by St. Matthew, translated into the *Grebo* Language. Printed at the Station Press of the American Board of Commissioners of Foreign Missions, Fair Hope.—12mo, Cape Palmas, (West Africa,) 1838. (E.)

Hauh Tibosa Ne Luke Kinena. THE GOSPEL according to St. Luke, translated into the *Grebo* Tongue by the Rev. John Payne, Missionary of the Protestant Episcopal Church at Cavalla, West Africa. Published by the American Bible Society.—16mo, New York, 1848. (E.)

Aposlebo ah Nunude. THE ACTS OF THE APOSTLES, translated into the *Grebo* Tongue by the Rev. John Payne, &c. Published by the American Bible Society.—18mo, New York, 1851. (E.)

THE GOSPEL according to St. Mark, in the *Grebo* Language. Without title page or date—18mo. Five copies. (E.)

GREEK VERSIONS.

NOVUM TESTAMENTUM, Graece et Latine; diligentia de Erasmi Roterod. Emendatissima et jam denuo ad multa exemplaria, tam impressa quam manuscripta, diligenta castigatum, et editum. Adjecta sunt argumenta cuisdam unà cum marginalibus concordantiis.—8vo, Basil, 1544. (H.)

NOVUM TESTAMENTUM, Graece et Latine.—12mo, Basil, 1544. (H.)

NOVUM TESTAMENTUM Graece. Ex Bibliotheca Regia. Ex officina Roberti Stephani.—32mo, Lutetiae, 1568. (H.)

This is the second volume of this edition of Stephens, commencing with the Epistle to the Romans.

NOVUM TESTAMENTUM Graecum, cum vulgata interpretatione Latina Graeci contextus lineis inserta, &c. Ben. Ariae Montani Hispalensis opera e verbo reddita, ac diverso characterum genere distincta in ejus est substituta locum.—12mo, Geneva, 1622. (H.)

NOVUM TESTAMENTUM Graece. Ex Typographia Regia. —Fol., Paris, 1642. (H.)

In this edition, published under the direction of Cardinal Mazarin, the various readings are placed at the end of the volume.

NOVUM TESTAMENTUM, Graeco Latinum. Interpretete Desiderio Erasmo, Roterodamo. Editio nova accuratissime recognita.—4to, Frankfort on the Mayne, 1672. (H.)

This edition is on large paper. The above copy is interleaved, and has numerous MS. notes, a portrait of Erasmus, and four other plates, purporting to represent the Evangelists.

NOVUM TESTAMENTUM Graece, &c., &c., opera ac studio Joannis Gregorii.—Fol., Oxford, 1703. (H.)

Formed on the edition of Fell, and has a preface, supposed to have been written by the bishop. "It would have been no loss," says Michaelis, "if this edition had never appeared."

NOVUM TESTAMENTUM Graece, cum lectionibus variantibus, &c., &c.—Fol., Rotterdam, 1710. (H.)

"This is a reimpression of Mill's Greek Testament, with the various readings of *twelve* additional MSS., *nine* of which were Persian. The principal advantage of this work is, that the readings which Mill had to insert in an Appendix, are incorporated in their proper places. The edition is inferior to Mill's in execution and accuracy. The Greek text is in two columns and distinct verses." [Dibdin's Greek and Latin Classics, vol. i., p. 147.]

NOVUM TESTAMENTUM Graecum; ita adornatum, ut Textus probatarum editionem Medullum mago variantum Lectionum in suas classes, distrutarum locorumque parallelorum delectum, &c. Jo. Alberto Bengelio. —4to, Tubingen, 1734. (H.)

The first edition of Bengel's New Testament. This volume contains the Apparatus Criticus. "His editions evince much conscientiousness, sound judgment, and good sense."—*Horne.*

NOVUM TESTAMENTUM Graecum, ad optimas quasque editiones, collatum et excusum, adjectis nonullis variantibus lectionibus, necnon Harmonia Evangeliorum et Chronotaxi Actuum Apostolicorum, accurante, M. Christiano Reineccius.—8vo, Leipsic, 1742. (H.)

This edition is recommended by Dibdin.

NOVUM TESTAMENTUM, Graece et Anglice.—2 vols. 12mo, Philadelphia, 1823. (H.)

This is Abner Kneeland's version.

NOVUM TESTAMENTUM Graecum, Griesbachii et Knappii denuo recognovit, dilectu varietatum lectionis testimoniis confirmatarum, adnotatione cum criticatum exigetica, &c., &c. Instruxit Joannes Severinus Vater.—8vo, Halle-Sax., 1824. (H.)

NOVUM TESTAMENTUM Graecum, ad Fidem optimorum librorum recensuit Joh. Aug. Henr. Tittmannus Prof. Editio Stereotypa.—8vo, Leipsic, 1824. (H.)

NOVUM TESTAMENTUM Graece, ex recensione Jo. Jac. Griesbachii, cum selecta lectionum varietate. Editio nova non tamen mutata. —8vo, Leipsic, 1825. (H.)

NOVUM TESTAMENTUM Graecum. (Knapp.)—2 vols. in 1, 8vo, Halle-Sax., 1829 (H.)

Novum Testamentum Graecum. (Sine anno.)—12mo. (H.)

The title page is wanting. It has the Greek Psalter prefixed.

See *Tregellos*, under "English Versions," for one of 1844.

Novum Testamentum Graece. Post Joh. Aug. Henr. Tittmannum, recognovit Augustus Hahn. Sumtibus et typis Caroli Tauchnitii.—12mo, Lipsiae, 1840. (H.)

Novum Testamentum Graece, ex Recensione Augusti Hahnii. Sumtibus et typis Caroli Tauchnitii.—16mo, Lipsiae, 1841. (H.)

Novum Testamentum Graece, (Antiq. et Hodiern.)—12mo, Halle-Sax., 1710. (H.)

This is an ancient and modern Greek Testament. The first London edition of the modern Greek Testament was in 1703, from the version of Myteline, 1638. The preface gave such offence to the Greek bishops and the Patriarch of Constantinople, that it was ordered to be burned. In 1705 it was reprinted, and the offensive passages of the preface omitted.

Novum Testamentum Graece, (Antiq. et Hodiern.)—12mo, London, 1810. (H.)

Novum Testamentum, (Modern Greek.)—12mo, London, 1814. (H.)

Novum Testamentum, (Modern Greek.)—12mo, St. Petersburgh, 1817. (H.)

Novum Testamentum, (Modern Greek.)—12mo, London, 1828. Two copies. (H.)

Novum Testamentum Graecum, (Hodiern.)—8vo, London, 1828. (H.)

Novum Testamentum Graece, (Antiq. et Hodiern.) Printed for the British and Foreign Bible Society.—8vo, London, 1830. Two copies. (H.)

The Book of Psalms, translated from the Hebrew. Printed for the British and Foreign Bible Society.—12mo, London, 1831. (H.)

Novum Testamentum Graecum, (Modern Greek.) Printed for the British and Foreign Bible Society.—8vo, London, 1832. Four copies. (H.)

Extracts from the Old Testament in Modern Greek.—12mo, Malta, 1833. (H.)

Novum Testamentum Graecum, (Modern Greek.) Printed for the American Bible Society. Second edition.—12mo, New York, 1835. (H.)

NOVUM TESTAMENTUM, (Modern Greek.) Printed for the American Bible Society. Third edition.—12mo, New York, 1836. (H.)

EXTRACTS from the New Testament in Modern Greek.—12mo, Malta, 1837. (H.)

NOVUM TESTAMENTUM, (Modern Greek.) Printed for the British and Foreign Bible Society.—12mo, Athens, 1838. (H.)

NOVUM TESTAMENTUM, (Modern Greek.)—8vo, Athens, 1844. (H.)

VETUS TESTAMENTUM Graecum, (Hodiern.) Printed for the British and Foreign Bible Society.—8vo, Oxford, 1850. (H.)

BIBLIA Graeca et Latina. (Basiliae ex officina Brylingeriana.)—8vo, Basil, 1852. (H.)

This edition is in five volumes. This copy is an odd volume containing the Book of Proverbs. It is printed in two columns, the outer column, the Latin; the inner, the Greek text, which is that of the Aldine edition; the Latin, of the Complutensian.

VETUS TESTAMENTUM Graecum, ex versione Septuaginta Interpretum. Juxta exemplar Vaticanum Romae Editum. Printed by Someren and Boorn.—12mo, Amsterdam, 1683. (H.)

This is a reprint of the Cambridge edition by John Field, without the Apocrypha and scholia.

VETUS TESTAMENTUM secund. Text. Alexandr. M.S. cum NOV. TEST. Published under the direction of the Moscow Bible Society. Russ. Synod. Press.—4to, Moscow, 1821. (H.)

The New Testament is from the edition of Cyril, patriarch of Constantinople, made in 1810.

The PSALMS of David, according to the Septuagint; to which is annexed, the New Testament in ancient Greek.—18mo. No date. (H.)

The book of PSALMS, in ancient Greek, from the original Hebrew.—12mo, London, 1831. (H.)

THE GREEK TESTAMENT, with English notes, critical, philological, and exegetical, &c., by Rev. S. T. Bloomfield, D.D. Fifth American edition.—2 vols. 8vo, Philadelphia and Boston, 1846. (H.)

GRAECO-TURKISH.

THE BOOK OF GENESIS, Graeco-Turkish. Mission Press of the Protestant Episcopal Church in the United States, established in Greece.—4to, Syra. Pamphlet. (D.)

VETUS TESTAMENTUM, Graeco-Turkish; or, the Turkish Old Testament in the Greek character.—8vo, Athens, 1838. (D.)

NOVUM TESTAMENTUM, Graeco-Turkish; or, the New Testament (Turkish) in the Greek character.—8vo, Athens, 1838. (D.)

See under *Turkish.*

GREENLAND.

Testamentuk Terssa, &c. THE NEW TESTAMENT of our Lord and Saviour Jesus Christ, translated into the *Greenland* Language by the Missionaries of the United Brethren. Printed for the Mission by the British and Foreign Bible Society.—8vo, London, 1822. (E.)

HAROTEE.

THE HOLY BIBLE, &c., translated from the originals into the *Harotee* Language, by the Serampore Missionaries. Vol. V., The New Testament. Printed at the Mission Press.—8vo, Serampore, 1821. (E.)

HAWAIIAN.

THE NEW TESTAMENT of our Lord and Saviour Jesus Christ, translated into the *Hawaiian* Language. The volume has no general title page. The following is the title to Matthew and the other Gospels, with change of name: Ka Eunnelio a Mataio; oia ka moo olelo hemolele no ko kakou haku e ola'e no Jesu Kristo, i laweia i olelo Hawii. Hookahi keia o ke pai ana. Rochester, N. Y. Paiia ma ka mea pai palapala a lumiki.—12mo, 1828. (E.)

This is the copy of the New Testament which *Haahumanu*, the late Queen of the Sandwich Islands, received with gratitude on her deathbed. A blank leaf of the volume bears the following inscription: "Presented by Kinau, the heiress of the late Queen, (its former possessor,) to the American Bible Society, in token of gratitude to that honourable body for its liberal aid in furnishing the Sandwich Islands with the precious Gospel of salvation. Oahu, January, 1834."

Ke kanoha hou a ko kakow hakueola i, a Jesu Kristo oia ka oleto hemolele no ke ola a na luna olelo i kakan ai Uaunu hila, mai ka olelo helene. Oahu; Na na misionari i pai 1835. The New Testament in the *Hawaiian* Language. Published by the Missionaries at the Sandwich Islands. —12mo, Oahu, 1835. (E.)

Ke kanoha hou a ko kakow hakuelaa' i, a Jesu Christo, &c. The New Testament, translated into the *Hawaiian* Language by the American Missionaries. Printed at the Mission Press.—12mo, Honolulu, 1837. (E.)

Ka palapala hemolele a Jehova ko kakou akua, &c. The Holy Bible, in the *Hawaiian* Language, by the American Missionaries.—12mo, Oahu, 1838. (E.)

It has three volumes in one, numbering about 2300 pages.

Ka palapala hemolele a Jehova ko kakou akua oke Kauoha Kahiko a me ke kanoha hou i unuhiia Mailoko Mai o na olelo Kahiko. Printed at the Mission Press.—8vo, Oahu, 1843. (E.)

The New Testament of this copy was printed at Honolulu.

HEBREW.

Biblia Hebraica; the Books of Proverbs, Job, Canticles, Ruth, Lamentations, Ecclesiastes, and Esther, with the Major and Minor Prophets, (Daniel excepted,) in the Hebrew Language.—2 vols. 32mo, Warsaw, 1566. (H.)

Biblia Hebraica, Johannis Simonis; with his analysis and explication of the Masoretic readings. Second edition.—8vo, Halle, 1766. (H.)

This copy has 16 duplicate pages of the Analysis prefixed to the work.

Biblia Hebraica, ex Recensione Aug. Hahnii, cum Vulgata interpretatione Latina, Denuo Edita. Sumtibus et typis Caroli Tauchnitii.—2 vols. 12mo, Lipsiæ, 1838. (H.)

Biblia Hebraica, ad optimas editiones inprimis Everardi van der Hooght, ex Recensione Aug. Hahnii expressa. Præfatus est Ern. Fr. Car. Rosenmüller. Sumtibus et typis Caroli Tauchnitii.—12mo, Lipsiæ, 1838. (H.)

Liber Psalmorum e minore Bibliorum Hebraicorum, &c. Sumtibus et typis Caroli Tauchnitii.—12mo, Lipsiæ, 1850. (H.)

Psalmi Hebraice cum versione Latina Vulgatae editionis. Sumtibus et typis Caroli Tauchnitii.—12mo, Lipsiæ, 1852. (H.)

The Book of Psalms, Hebrew and English. Printed and published by Karl Tauchnitz.—12mo, Leipsig, 1852. (H.)

David's Psalmer, Hebreisk och Svensk. Trykt och förlagt af Karl Tauchnitz.—12mo, Leipsig, 1852. (H.)

Psalmi Hebraice cum Septuaginta interpretum versione Graeca. Sumtibus et typis Caroli Tauchnitii.—12mo, Lipsiæ, 1852. (H.)

David's Psalmer, Hebraisk og Dansk. Trykt og forlagt af Karl Tauchnitz.—12mo, Leipsig, 1853. (H.)

Biblia Hebraica; the Holy Scriptures of the Old Testament in the original Hebrew; without the vowel points, after the text of Kennicott, with the chief various readings selected from his collation of Hebrew MSS., from that of De Rossi, and from the ancient versions. With English Notes, &c., selected from ancient and modern Biblical critics. By B. Boothroyd.—2 vols. 4to, 1810-1816. (H.)

A "commodious, correct, and truly philological edition of the sacred text in the original tongue," and is highly recommended to the Hebrew scholar.

Novum Testamentum Hebraice. The New Testament, &c., in the Hebrew Language.—8vo, London, 1817. (H.)

The Book of the Law, the Prophets, and the Psalms, or the Old Testament Scriptures, in Hebrew and German.—2 vols. 12mo, London, 1841–2. (H.)

The Pentateuch; or, the Five Books of the Law, in the original Hebrew.—5 vols. 4to, Vienna, 1840. (H.)

This work is in a case.

The Hebrew and Hebrew-Spanish Psalter, in parallel columns. Printed at the expense of the American Bible Society.—4to, Constantinople, 1836. Two copies. (H.)

Biblia Hebraica, secundum editiones Jos. Athiae, Johannis Leusden, Jo. Simonis, aliorumque imprimis Everardi van der Hooght, recensuit sectionum propheti earum recensum, et explicationem clavemque Masorethicum et Rabbinicum addidit, Augustus Hahn. Editio stereotypa Quartiem.—8vo, Leipsic, 1839. (H.)

Biblia Hebraica et Germanica; the Holy Bible, with a German translation.—2 vols. 8vo, London. (H.)

The Book of Psalms, in *Hebrew* and *English*, arranged in parallel columns. Bagster & Sons.—8vo, London, 1846. (H.)

Biblia Hebraica; or, the Hebrew Scriptures of the Old Testament, without points, after the text of Kennicott, &c., accompanied with English notes, critical, philological, and explanatory, &c., by B. Boothroyd. —2 vols. in 1, 4to, Pontefract, (no date.) (H.)

HINDEE, (India.)

The Prophecies of Isaiah, in the *Hindee* Language.—8vo, Serampore, 1812. (E.)

The Pentateuch; or, the Five Books of the Law, in *Hindee*.—8vo, Serampore, 1812. (E.)

NOVUM TESTAMENTUM; the New Testament, in the *Hindee* Language, translated from the originals by the Serampore Missionaries: being vol. V. of the entire Bible. Printed at the Mission Press.—8vo, Serampore, 1821. (E.)

HINDI.

The Epistles of Paul to the Romans and Corinthians; translated into the *Hindi* Dialect. Presbyterian Mission Press. Printed at the expense of the American Bible Society.—12mo, Lodiana, 1841. (E.)

The Book of Deuteronomy, in the *Hindi* Dialect. Presbyterian Mission Press.—12mo, Lodiana, 1843. (E.)

PSALTERIUM DAVIDIS; the Book of Psalms, in *Hindi*. Presbyterian Mission Press.—12mo, Allahabad, 1843. (E.)

The Book of Deuteronomy and the Book of Daniel; translated into *Hindi*. Presbyterian Mission Press.—16mo, Lodiana, 1843. (E.)

The Books of Genesis and Exodus, in the *Hindi* Tongue. Revised by the Hindi Sub-committee of the North India Bible Society. Presbyterian Mission Press.—8vo, Allahabad, 1850. (E.)

BIBLIA SACRA; the Holy Bible, in the *Hindi* Language. Translated from the Hebrew. Vol. I. Presbyterian Mission Press.—8vo, Allahabad, 1851. (E.)

HINDOSTANEE, (India.)

The Book of Proverbs, in *Hindostanee*.—8vo. (E.)

THE GOSPEL according to St. John, in the *Hindostanee* Language.—8vo. Six copies. (E.)

THE GOSPEL according to St. Matthew, in *Hindostanee* and *English*. Printed for the Calcutta Auxiliary Bible Society, Hindostanee Press.—8vo, Calcutta, 1819. Two copies. (E.)

NOVUM TESTAMENTUM, HIND.; the New Testament, &c., translated into the *Hindostanee* Language from the original Greek, by Rev. Henry Martyn; revised with the assistance of Mirza Fitrit and other learned natives. Printed for the British and Foreign Bible Society.—8vo, London, 1819. (E.)

THE PENTATEUCH; or, Five Books of Moses, translated into the *Hindostanee* Language from the original Hebrew, under the patronage of the Calcutta Bible Society. Mission Press.—8vo, Serampore, 1822. (E.)

VETUS TESTAMENTUM, HIND.; the Old Testament, translated from the original Hebrew into the *Hindostanee* Language. Vol. I., containing Genesis to 2 Kings, (inclusive.) Calcutta Auxiliary Bible Society.—4to, Calcutta, 1829. (E.)

NOVUM TESTAMENTUM, HIND.; the New Testament, translated from the original Greek into the Hindostanee Language. Printed for the Calcutta Auxiliary Bible Society.—4to, Serampore, 1829. (E.)

THE GOSPEL by St. Matthew, translated from the Greek by the American Baptist Missionaries. Baptist Mission Press.—8vo, Calcutta, 1837. Pamphlet. (E.)

THE GOSPEL according to St. Mark, in *Hindostanee*, translated as above. Baptist Mission Press.—8vo, Calcutta, 1837. Pamphlet. (E.)

THE GOSPEL by St. Luke, in Hindostanee, translated as above. Baptist Mission Press.—8vo, Calcutta, 1837. (E.)

The Four Gospels and the Acts of the Apostles, translated from the Greek into *Hindostanee* as above. Printed at the Baptist Mission Press for the American and Foreign Bible Society.—8vo, Calcutta, 1838. (E.)

THE GOSPEL according to St. Luke, in Hindostanee. American Mission Press.—8vo, Lodiana, 1838. (E.)

THE GOSPEL by St. John, in *Hindostanee*. American Mission Press for the American Bible Society.—8vo, Lodiana, 1839. (E.)

THE NEW TESTAMENT, &c., in the *Hindostanee* Language, translated by the Calcutta Baptist Missionaries with native assistants. Baptist Mission Press for the American and Foreign Bible Society.—8vo, Calcutta, 1839. (E.)

THE ACTS of the Apostles, in *Hindostanee*. American Mission Press.—8vo, Lodiana, 1839. Two copies. (E.)

The Epistle of St. Paul to the ROMANS, in *Hindostanee*. Printed at the American Mission Press for the American Bible Society.—12mo, Lodiana, 1840. Two copies. (E.)

The Epistles to the PHILIPPIANS, COLOSSIANS, and THESSALONIANS, in *Hindostanee*. American Presbyterian Mission Press for the American Bible Society.—12mo, Lodiana, 1841. Two copies. (E.)

The Book of PSALMS, in *Hindostanee*. American Presbyterian Mission Press for the American Bible Society.—8vo, Lodiana, 1841. Two copies. (E.)

The Prophecies of ISAIAH, in *Hindostanee*. American Presbyterian Mission Press.—12mo, Lodiana, 1842. (E.)

The Book of Deuteronomy, in *Hindostanee.* American Presbyterian Mission Press for the American Bible Society.—12mo, Lodiana, 1842. (E.)

The Gospel by St. Luke and St. John, the Acts of the Apostles, and the Epistle to the Romans, in *Hindostanee.* American Presbyterian Mission Press for the American Bible Society.—8vo, Lodiana, 1845. (E.)

The Gospel according to St. Matthew, in *Hindostanee.* Printed at the American Presbyterian Mission Press for the American Bible Society.—12mo, Lodiana, 1846. (E.)

HINDUEE.

The New Testament, &c., altered from Martyn's Oordoo translation into the *Hinduee* Language, by Rev. William Bowley, under the patronage of the Calcutta Auxiliary Bible Society. Church Mission Press.—8vo, Calcutta, 1826. (E.)

The Holy Scriptures, translated into the *Hinduee* Language, by Rev. William Bowley, as above. Vol. I.—8vo, Calcutta, 1826. (E.)

The Book of Proverbs, in *Hinduee.*—8vo. Pamphlet. (E.)

The Gospel according to St. Matthew, in the *Hinduee* Language.—12mo. Pamphlet. (E.)

HUNGARIAN. (See Magyar.)

ICELANDIC.

Biblia, tad er, Aull heilang Rituing u elangd a Islendsku; the Bible, that is, all the Holy Scriptures, translated into the Icelandic Tongue. Printed for the British and Foreign Bible Society, according to the edition (Copenhagen) of 1747.—8vo, Copenhagen, 1813. (E.)

INDIAN. (See American Indian.)

INDO-PORTUGUESE. (See Portuguese.)

IRISH.

Tiomnaidh Nuadh, &c.; or, the Irish Bible. Roman character.—12mo, London, 1807. (E.)

Tiomna Nuadh ar Dtig hearna agus ar Slanuig heora Josa Criosd, &c., Re Hcilliam O'Domhnuill. The New Testament, in the *Irish* Language. Roman character.—12mo, Shacklewell, 1813. (E.)

Tiomnadh Nuadh; the New Testament, in the *Irish* Language. Roman character.—12mo, Edinburgh, 1813. (E.)

An Biobla Naomhtha; the Holy Bible, in the *Irish* Language. Roman character. Printed for the British and Foreign Bible Society. —8vo, London, 1817. (E.)

Tiomna Nuadh; the New Testament, in the *Irish* Language. Vernacular character.—12mo, London, 1818. (E.)

Tpsaltair; the Book of Psalms, in the *Irish* Language. Vernacular character.—12mo, London, 1825. (E.)

Leabhuir an Tsean Tiomna, &c.; the Holy Bible, in the *Irish* Language. Vernacular character.—8vo, Dublin, 1827. (D.)

An Diobla Naomhtha; the Holy Bible, in the *Irish* Tongue. Vernacular character.—18mo, Dublin, 1830. (E.)

The Book of Genesis, in the *Irish* vernacular. Sine loco, sine anno.—18mo. (E.)

Tiomna Nuadh; the New Testament, in the *Irish* Language. Vernacular character.—18mo, London, 1830. (E.)

Tiomna Nuadh; the New Testament, in the *Irish* Language, with various readings from the 4to edition of 1681–5. Vernacular character.—18mo, London, 1830. Two copies. (E.)

Leabhuir an Tsean Tiomna, &c.; the Old and New Testaments, in the *Irish* Language, with various readings, &c., as above. Vernacular character.—12mo, London, 1830. (E.)

See also under *Gaelic*.

ITALIAN.

Il Nuevo ed Eterno Testamento di Giesu Christo. Per Giovanni di Tornes, e Guillelmo Gazeio.—32mo, Lyons, 1616. (F.)

This Testament is printed in Italic type. It has no verses, but is divided into sections, marked with the letters of the alphabet. It contains 94 engravings.

La Sacro-Santa Biblia in Lingua Italiana, cive Il Vecchio e Nuovo Testamento nella purità della Lingua volgare, moderna e corretta correspondente per tutto al Testo fondamentale vero, distinta per versetti a pro della Gioventii, e stampata con lettere molto leggibili, à pro di quei, che sono d'età avanzata, &c. Da Mattia d'Erberg, &c.—Fol., Nuremberg, 1721. (F.)

A revised edition of Diodati's version. Both the Old and the New Testaments have an engraved frontispiece; that to the New Testament is very fanciful, and approaching very near to a violation of the second commandment.

Il Nuovo Testamento del nostro Signore Geso Christo. Edizione Stereotypa.—12mo, Shacklewell, 1813. (F.)

Il Nuovo Testamento, secondo la Volgata, tradotto in Lingua Italiana da Monsignor Antonio Martini.—12mo, London, 1818. (F.)

Il Nuovo Testamento, &c. The New Testament, translated from the Vulgate into the Italian Language, by Antonio Martini.—12mo, Firenze, 1819. (F.)

La Sacra Bibbia, tradotta de Giovanni Diodati. Edizione Londnèse Rive duta da Giambattista Rolandi, &c.—8vo, London, 1819. (F.)

In this edition, the Old Testament and the Apocrypha have no contents at the head of the chapters; they are inserted, however, in the New Testament.

Il Nuovo Testamento, secondo la Volgata, tradotto in Lingua Italiana da M. Antonio Martini, &c. Scrupolosamente Riscontato de G. B. Rolandi colla versione originale publicata in Toino.—12mo, London, 1821. (F.)

A Catholic version.

La Sacra Bibbia, contenente l'antico ed il Nuovo Testamento; tradotta da Giovanni Diodati. Stampata per la Societa Biblica.—8vo, Basil, 1822. (F.)

Psalterium; hoc est Psalmorum Liber, excerptis e Bibliis Sacris a Sixto V. P. M. recognitis.

Libro dei Salmi. Tradotto in Italiano secondo il Testo della Volgata, da M. Martini, &c.—8vo, London, 1822. (F.)

The Latin and Italian Psalter.

LA SACRA BIBBIA, che contiene Il Vechio e Il Nuovo Testamento. Tradotta in Lingua Italiana da Giovanni Diodati.—24mo, London, 1841. (F.)

JAPANESE.

The Gospel according to St. John, in the *Japanese* Language.—4to. Pamphlet. Three copies. (E.)

JAVANESE.

The New Testament, in the *Javanese* Language.—8vo. (E.)

KARELIAN, (Russia.)

The Gospel according to St. Matthew, translated into the *Karelian* Tongue.—8vo, 1820. (E.)

This dialect is spoken in a province about 50 miles northwest of St. Petersburgh.

See *Slavonic*.

KAREN.

SGAN KAREN; The Gospel by St. John, in the *Karen* Language.—8vo. Pamphlet. (E.)

KASHMEERA, (India.)

THE HOLY BIBLE, containing the Old and New Testaments, translated from the originals into the *Kashmeera* Language, by the Serampore Missionaries. Vol. V., The New Testament. Mission Press.—8vo, Serampore, 1821. (E.)

KAITHI'-HINDI'.

The Book of Psalms and the Book of Proverbs, in the *Kaithi'-Hindi'* Language. Presbyterian Mission Press for the Calcutta Auxiliary Bible Society.—12mo, Allahabad, 1845. (E.)

The Books of Genesis and Exodus, in *Hindi'-Kaithi'*. Presbyterian Mission Press for the Calcutta Auxiliary Bible Society.—12mo, Allahabad, 1845. (E.)

The Epistles of Paul to the Romans and the Hebrews, in *Kaithi'-Hindi'*. Presbyterian Mission Press for the American Bible Society.—8vo, Allahabad, 1846. Pamphlet. (E.)

The Gospel of Luke, in *Kaithi'-Hindi'*.—8vo. Pamphlet. (E.)

The New Testament, in *Kaithu-Hindu*.—8vo. (E.)

The Four Gospels and the Acts of the Apostles, in *Kaithu-Hindui*.—8vo. (E.)

KINIKA.

Euangelio za Avioandika Lukas; the Gospel according to St. Luke, translated into *Kinika* by Rev. John Lewis Krapf, Phil. Dr. Printed at the American Mission Press.—12mo, Bombay, 1848. (E.)

The Kinika language is used south of Abyssinia, towards Zanzebar.

KUN-KUNA, (India.)

The Holy Bible, containing the Old and New Testaments, translated from the originals into the *Kun-Kuna* Language. Vol. V., containing the New Testament. Mission Press.—12mo, Serampore, 1818. (E.)

LAPONIAN or LAPONESE, (Lapland.)

Adda Testament Tate Ailes Tjalogest Same Kialei Puoltetum; the New Testament, in the *Laponian* Language.—8vo, Herno Sand, 1811. (E.)

LATIN.

Biblia Latina Vulgata. Nicolai Jenson.—Fol., Venice, 1476. (H.)

As this is the oldest printed copy of the Sacred Scriptures in the Society's collection, and nearly the oldest *ever* printed,* the following description by Dr. Dibdin, of a copy of the same edition on vellum, belonging to Earl Spencer, is here given; which agrees exactly with the present copy, with but one or two exceptions: viz., 1st, the omission of a splendid *illumination* at the beginning of the Pentateuch, representing the ALMIGHTY; and the substitution of one less pretending, but of the same size, representing the *Temptation* of our first parents in Eden; and, 2d, its being on *paper* instead of vellum. The volume "begins on the recto of the first leaf, sig. A 2, with the running title 'PROLOGUS.' Beneath, 'INCIPIT EPLA SACTI HIERONYMI AD PAULINU PBRZ, DE OIBQ DIUINE HISTORIE LIBRIS CAPBZ I.' The Prologue occupies five pages, ending on the recto of sig. A 4. On the reverse is St. Jerome's Preface to the Pentateuch. On the recto of the ensuing leaf, A 5, begins the Pentateuch. The volume has running titles throughout. There are two sets of signatures; the first in small Gothic (or black) letter, extending to 4; the second, in capitals, to X 7. There are 10 leaves to each signature, except a few of the latter. Q has 12 leaves; on the reverse of the last of which, at the bottom, is the Colophon:

Biblia impressa Venitiis opera atqz impensa Nicolai Jenson Gallici MccccLxxvi.

The '*Interpretationes Hebraicorum nominum*,' &c., commences on the recto of the ensuing leaf, sig. R. This table is printed in two columns, and concludes on the recto of sig. X 7, in tens, except U, which has only eight leaves:

Expliciunt Interpretatio-
nes hebraicoru nominu
Laus deo.

A blank leaf in sig. H divides the Old from the New Testament. The heads of the chapters are Roman capitals. Seemiller says, the entire work consists of 470 leaves. A full page contains 52 lines. According to the same authority, and to De Bure, there should be a leaf after the preceding Colophon, containing 'Registrum Biblie,' which is wanting in the present copy." [Bibliotheca Spenceriana, vol. i., p. 32.] To this description of the work by Dr. Dibdin, it may be added, that the present copy is complete, having that missing leaf and "Register," and agreeing in all the aforementioned particulars with the description. Like the previous editions, the Book of Psalms has the running title of "PSALMISTA," and number 171 the 119th, being distinctly lettered in each of its 22 sections, and running from the 118th to the 139th number inclusive. The capitals are all illuminated, some of them gilded. "A copy of the *first* edition of the Latin Vulgate Bible (Jerome's), belonging to the late Mr. James Perry, was purchased by His Royal Highness the Duke of Sussex for 160 guineas." [Library Companion, by Dibdin, p. 13, note.] "A copy of this edition on vellum was purchased at the sale of M. Paris for £59 17*s*., and was sold again to the Duke of Devonshire for £168." [Biblioth. Sussex., vol. i., p. 322-3.]

BIBLIA SACRA LATINA cu concordantiis Veteris et Novi Testamenti. Sanctus Hieronymus interpres Biblie. Anth. Koberger.—Fol., Nuremberg, 1501. (H.)

This edition of the Vulgate follows the Frobenian of 1495. On the title page, in a woodcut, are two figures of St. Jerome, one sitting, the other kneel-

* The first edition of the Holy Scriptures, and, as is supposed, the first book printed with moveable metallic types, was the Latin Bible, printed by John Guttenberg, (the inventor of printing,) A.D. 1450-5, in 2 vols., fol., at Moguntiae.

ing, under which are the verses: "*Simachus atq: Theodotion vel septuaginta*," &c., as in the edition of 1495. Gabriel Bruno's "Alphabetical Table of the Books of the Old and New Testaments" follows, and is succeeded by an exhortation to the lovers of sacred literature; a metrical order of the several books, &c. This Bible (preceded by the Prologue of St. Jerome) is printed in two columns, in a large Gothic (or black) letter. The chapters are numbered, and divided into lesser sections, and the parallel places are put in the margin. The capital letters are *written* in with red and blue ink. At the end of the Apocalypse is an epilogue, closing as follows: "Per Anthonium Koberger, Nurembergae, impressa finit feliciter. Anno post Xri nativitate rno supra Millesimu 7 quinquetesimu die 24 mensis Marcii."

BIBLIA LATINA, cumpleno apparatu summariorum Concordantiorum et quadruplicis repertorii sive indicii; numerique foliorum distinctione tersissime ac verissime impressa. Impressum est per Magistrum Jacobum Sacon.—Fol., Lugduni, 1509. (H.)

Printed in a handsome Gothic letter, with the usual preliminary matter. The margin is filled with MS. notes.

BIBLIA LATINA, &c., (ut supra.) Additi sunt Eusbii pamphib Cesariensis Epidecem canones; et quibus que apud quatuor Evangelistes, vel eadem vel vicina vel sola sunt clarissime apparuit, &c. Impressa Johanne Froben de Hammelburg.—Fol., Basil, 1514. (H.)

Printed in a fair Gothic type, with parallel passages in the margin. Under most of the principal words are written, in a small hand, their definitions in German.

BIBLIA LATINA, VULGATA, cu concordantiis Veteris et Novi Testamenti, et Sacrorum canonum; nec non it additionibus in marginibus varietatis diversos textuum; ac etiam canonibus antiquis quatuor evangeliorum. Novissime autem addite sunt concordantie et Vinginti libris Josephi de Antiquitatibus et Bello Judaico excerpte. Impressa Jacobum Sacon; Expesis notabilis viri Antonii Koberger Nurebergensis, &c.—Fol., Lugduni, 1520. (H.)

Two copies. This edition has many curious woodcuts.

SACRA BIBLIA ad LXX. interpretum fidem diligentissime tralata Basileæ, per Andream Cratandrum.—8vo, Basle, 1526. (H.)

This copy is in oak binding, and has been preserved with great care.

BIBLIA LATINA; ad vetustissima exemplaria nunc recens castigata, Hebraea, Chaldaea, Graeca et Latina nomina virorum, mulierum, populorum, idolorum, urbium, fluviorum, montium, ceterorumque locorum quae in Bibliis loquntur, restituta cum Latina interpretatione, ac locorum e Cosmographis descriptione, &c., &c. Ex officina Bartholomaei Gravii Typographia.—Fol., Louvanii, 1547. (H.)

"This is the first Louvain edition according to the recension of Hentenius, as approved by the Doctors of Louvain, and is of very considerable rarity. In this edition, the Vulgate is said to have been corrected by *thirty* MSS. The chapters are numbered, but not the verses. The privilege for printing this edition, granted by Charles V., is in Latin, French, and German.

BIBLIA SACRA, Veteris et Novi Testamenti, juxta Vulgatam, quam dicunt, editionem Joannis Benedicti, Parisiensis, Theologi industria accuraté recognita et emendata, Annorumque a Mundo condito ad Christum usque natu supputatione illustrata, &c., &c. Apud haeredes Carolae Guillard Viduae quondam Claudii Chenallonii.—Fol., Paris, 1558. (H.)

This is the fourth Benedictine edition, and was prohibited. [See Index Lib. Prohib., 1667.]

BIBLIA, VETERIS AC NOVI TESTAMENTI, summa fide ac studio singulari, cum aliorum doctissimorum interpretum, tam vero in primis S. Pagnini ac Fr. Vatab. opera ita ex Hebraeis, Graecis, fontubus expressa, et latinitate donata, veterum insuper codicum aliquot collatione emendata, ut nihil relictum sid quod a pio et sacrae lectionis studioso desiderari posse videatur, &c.—Fol., Basil, 1564. (H.)

This edition of the Latin Bible is very scarce. It is found in the list of books prohibited by the Roman Church. In the Printer's Address it is stated that the Old Testament is Pagnini's version, and the New Testament, the translation of Theodore Beza. Most of the collateral matter is taken from the editions of R. Stephens. The titles of the books are in Hebrew and Latin, or Greek and Latin, according to the translation from one or the other.

TESTAMENTI VETERIS BIBLIA SACRA; sive Libri Canonici priscae Judaeorum, Ecclesiae a Deo Traditi, Latini recens ex Hebraeo facti, brevibusque Scholiis illustrati, ab Immanuelé Tremellio et Francisco Junio. Accesserunt Libri Apocryphi, &c. Secunda cura Francisci Junii.—4to, Geneva, 1590. (H.)

Francis Junius was the editor of this edition, and he made many alterations in the Old Testament. His notes are distinguished by the letter F. The New Testament, which is from the London edition of 1585, has additions from the fourth edition of Beza's New Testament, 1588. Notes are added by Tornesius.

TESTAMENTI VETERIS BIBLIA SACRA; sive Libri Canonici priscae Judaeorum, &c., &c., (as above.)—Fol., Hanover, 1603. (H)

This edition was approved by the Protestant churches, and is still esteemed for its simplicity, perspicuity, and fidelity.

TESTAMENTI VETERIS, &c., &c.—Fol., Hanover, 1603. (H.)

A duplicate copy, (interleaved.)

LIBER PSALMORUM DAVIDIS REGIS ET PROPHETE, ex Arabico Idiomate in Latinum translatus. A Victorio Scialae et Gabriele Lioniti, Edeniensi Maronitis, e Monte Libano, Prof., &c., &c. Stephanus Paulinus, Typo. —4to, Rome, 1614. (H.)

BIBLIA SACRA, VULGATAE, editionis Sixti Quinti, Pont. Max. IVSSV recognita atque edita. D'Villiers, Typo.—8vo, Lugduni, 1627. (H.)

Prefixed is a Preface to the Reader; the Decree of the Council of Trent; and at the end are Jerome's Prologues and an Index Biblicus.

BIBLIA SACRA, sive Testamentum Vetus, ab Im. Tremellio et Fr. Junio, ex Hebraeo Latini redditum; et TESTAMENTUM NOVUM, a Theod.

Beza e Graeco in Latinum versum. Indefessus agendo.—12mo, Amsterdam, 1628. (H.)

This is a Protestant version.

TESTAMENTI VETERIS BIBLIA SACRA; sive Libri Canonici priscae Judaeorum, &c., ab Immanuele Tremellio et Francisco Junio, &c., cum Indice et Notas V. T. triplica, Hebraeo, Graeco et Latino.—Fol., Geneva, 1630. (H.)

This edition corresponds with that edited by Junius in 1617, and has the Index by William Baudart.

BIBLIA SACRA. Tremellius and Junius. Printed by the Stationers' Company.—12mo, London, 1655. (H.)

The New Testament is that of Beza. It has Sternhold and Hopkins's metrical version of the Psalms. The title pages are both wanting.

NOVUM TESTAMENTUM Domini Nostri Jesu Christi. Interprete Theodore Beza.—12mo, London, 1735. (H.)

NOVUM TESTAMENTUM, juxta exemplar Joannis Milii accuratissime impressum. Editio Prim. a Americana. Excudebat Isaiah Thomas, Jr.—12mo, Wigomiae, (Mass.), 1800. (H.)

NOVUM TESTAMENTUM, Vulgatae editionis, &c. Edente Dr. F. F. Fleck. Sumtibus et typis Caroli Tauchnitii.—12mo, Lipsiae, 1840. (H.)

LETTISH or LIVONIAN, (Russian.)

Ta Jauna Derriba, Muhsu Kunga Jesus Kristus. The New Testament of our Lord Jesus Christ, in the *Lettish* Language.—8vo, 1816. (E.)

Two copies. This dialect is spoken 200 miles southwest of St. Petersburgh.

LITHUANIAN. (See Samogitian.)

MAGYAR or HUNGARIAN.

Uq Testamentum, azaz A'mi urunk Jesus Krisztusnak ujszöbelsége Magyar Nyelore Fordetotta Karoli Gaspar Koszegen. THE NEW TESTAMENT, that is, the Book of our Lord Jesus Christ, translated into the *Magyar* or *Hungarian* Language, by Charles Gaspar.—12mo, 1846. (D.)

SZENT BIBLIA AZAZ; or, the Holy Bible, in the *Magyar* or *Hungarian* Language.—8vo, 1850. Two copies. (D.)

MAHRATTA or MURAT-HEE.

THE GOSPEL according to St. Matthew, translated into the *Mahratta* Language.—12mo, Bombay, 1818. Pamphlet. (E.)

THE NEW TESTAMENT, &c., in the *Mahratta* Language. —8vo. (E.)

THE NEW TESTAMENT, &c., translated from the original Greek into the *Murat-hee* Language, by the American Missionaries. Second edition. Printed for the Bombay Auxiliary Bible Society.—8vo, Bombay, 1830. Three copies. (E.)

THE NEW TESTAMENT, &c., translated from the original Greek into *Mara'thi'*. Printed at the Ahmednuggur Mission Press.—12mo, Bombay, 1850. (E.)

THE NEW TESTAMENT, &c., translated from the original Greek into *Mara'thi'*. American Mission Press.—8vo, Bombay, 1851. (E.)

MALAY.

ELKITAB; eja itu, Segala Surat Perdj an dj i an Lama Dan Baharuw. The Holy Bible, in the *Malay* Language. Roman characters.—2 vols. 4to, Amsterdam, 1733. (E.)

ELKITAB, &c. The Malay Bible, in *Arabic* characters.—4to, Serampore, 1817. (D.)

TESTAMENTUM Malaice. The New Testament, in the *Malay* Language. Roman characters. Printed for the British and Foreign Bible Society.—8vo, London, 1818. (E.)

NOVUM TESTAMENTUM, Malaice; Cura et sumtibus Societatis quae Bibliis per omnes gentes per vulgandis operam dat. Ementatius Edition.—8vo, Harlem, 1820. (E.)

ELKITAB, &c.; or, the Malay Bible. Roman characters. —8vo, London, 1821. (D.)

NOVUM TESTAMENTUM, Malaice; or, the New Testament, &c., in the *Malay* Language. Revised edition. Printed at the Mission Press for the British and Foreign Bible Society.—8vo, Singapore, 1831. (E.)

THE GOSPEL according to St. John, translated into the *Malay* Language. Arabic characters. Press of the American Mission.—8vo, Singapore, 1837. (E.)

This version was made by Rev. W. Robinson, an English Baptist missionary, and first printed by him at Bencoolen, on the west coast of Sumatra, in 1823. He was deemed an accomplished scholar. This edition is a reprint from the one mentioned above, at the expense of the American Bible Society.

MANDJUR.

THE GOSPEL according to St. Matthew, in the *Mandjur* Language.—4to. Pamphlet. (E.)

This language is spoken northwest of China, and reads downwards.

MANKS, (Isle of Man.)

CONAANT NOA nyn Jiarn as Saualtagh Yeesy Creest. The New Testament, &c., in the *Manks* Dialect. Printed for the British and Foreign Bible Society.—12mo, London, 1815. (E.)

Yn Vible Casherick ny yn chenn chonaunt as yn Conaant Noa, &c. The Holy Bible, containing the Old and New Testaments, in the *Manks* or Gaelic Dialect. Printed for the British and Foreign Bible Society.—8vo, London, 1819. (E.)

See, also, under *Gaelic* and *Irish*.

MOLDAVIAN or WALLACHIAN.

NOVY TESTAMENT, ey Domiyni Nostri, Jisus Christos. The New Testament of our Lord Jesus Christ, in the *Moldavian* Language. Published by the Russian Bible Society.—8vo, St. Petersburgh, 1817. (E.)

NOVA TECTAMENT au Domnouoi Chi Mintuitorouoi Nostro ESuS Christos. The New Testament of our Lord and Saviour Jesus Christ, translated into the *Moldavian* or *Wallachian* Language. Printed for the British and Foreign Bible Society.—8vo, Smyrna, 1838. Two copies. (E.)

MONGOLIAN, (Tartar.)

BIBLIA SACRA; the Holy Scriptures, in the *Mongolian* tongue. In 6 Parts.—4to, St. Petersburgh, 1835. (E.)

This copy is imperfect. The Mongolian dialect prevails west of China.

The Books of Genesis, Exodus, Leviticus, and Numbers, translated into the *Mongolian* Language.—2 vols. 4to, St. Petersburgh, 1835. (E.)

The Book of Psalms, in the *Mongolian* Tongue. Printed for and at the expense of the New York Bible Society.—12mo, St. Petersburgh, 1836. (E.)

The Book of Psalms, &c., (as above.)—4to. Pamphlet. (F.)

MOULTAN or WUCH, (Central India.)

The Holy Bible, containing the Old and New Testaments, translated from the Originals into the *Moultan* Language by the Serampore Missionaries. Vol. II., containing the New Testament. Printed at the Mission Press.—8vo, Serampore, 1819. (E.)

Two copies. This language is spoken 600 miles northwest of Calcutta.

MORDVINIAN. (See Russ.)

MPONGWE, (African.)

The Gospel according to St. Matthew, in the *Mpongwe* Language. Press of the American Board of Commissioners of Foreign Missions.—12mo, Gaboon, (Western Africa,) 1850. (E.)

The Gospel according to St. John, translated into the *Mpongwe* Language by the Missionaries of the American Board of Commissioners for Foreign Missions, Gaboon, Western Africa. Published by the American Bible Society.—12mo, New York, 1852. (E.)

NEGRO-ENGLISH, (Surinam.)

Da Njoe Testament va wi Masra en helpiman Jesus Christus. The New Testament of our Lord and Saviour Jesus Christ, translated into the *Negro-English* Language by the Missionaries of the "United Brethren." Printed for the Mission by the British and Foreign Bible Society.—8vo, London, 1829. (E.)

NEPALA, (Central India.)

The Holy Bible, containing the Old and New Testaments, translated from the Originals into the *Nepala* Language by the Serampore Missionaries. Vol. V., containing the New Testament. Printed at the Mission Press.—8vo, Serampore, 1821.

ORENBURGH. (See Tartar.)

OORDOO, (India.)

The Book of Genesis, translated into the *Oordoo* Language.—8vo, Calcutta. (E.)

The Book of Psalms, in *Oordoo*.—8vo, Calcutta. (E.)

The Book of Proverbs, in *Oordoo*.—8vo. Pamphlet. (E.)

ORISSA or URIYA, (Northern India.)

The Historical Books of the Old Testament, translated into the *Orissa* Language.—8vo, Serampore. (E.)

The Prophetical Books of the Old Testament, in the *Orissa* Language.—8vo. (E.)

OTAHEITAN. (See Taheitan.)

PERSIAN.

Novum Testamentum, Domini et Salvatoris, nostri, Jesu Christi; e Graeco in Persicum Linguam, a viro Reverendo Henrico Martyno, translatum, in urbe Schiras; nunc vero cura et sumptibus Societatis Biblicae Ruthenicae, Typis datum.—4to, St. Petersburgh, 1815. (E.)

Two copies. This Testament was printed under the inspection of Sir Gore Ousely.

The Book of Psalms, translated into the *Persian* Language.—8vo, Calcutta, 1816. (E.)

The Prophecies of Isaiah, in the *Persian* Language.—8vo. (E.)

THE NEW TESTAMENT, &c., translated from the original Greek into *Persian* at Scheeraz, by the Rev. Henry Martyn, B.D., with the assistance of Meerza Sueyid Ulee of Sheeraz. Printed at the Hindostanee Press for the British and Foreign Bible Society.—8vo, Calcutta, 1816. (E.)

The Book of Genesis, in the *Persian* Language, from Mirza Jaffier's version, by Prof. Lee.—8vo, Calcutta, 1827. (E.)

THE NEW TESTAMENT, &c., translated from the original Greek into *Persian*, by Rev. H. Martyn. Third edition. Printed for the British and Foreign Bible Society.—8vo, London, 1827. (E.)

THE PENTATEUCH, or, Five Books of Moses, in the *Persian* Language.—4to, Calcutta, 1828. (E.)

THE NEW TESTAMENT, &c., translated into *Persian*, by Rev. H. Martyn, &c. Printed at the Church Mission Press.—8vo, Calcutta, 1828. (E.)

The Holy Scriptures of the Old Testament, translated by Rev. William Glen. Printed for the British and Foreign Bible Society.—2 vols. 8vo, Edinburgh, 1845. (E.)

This translation is printed in the same style and size as the Edinburgh edition of H. Martyn's Persian New Testament.

THE NEW TESTAMENT, &c., translated into *Persian*, by Rev. H. Martyn. Printed for the British and Foreign Bible Society by T. Constable.—8vo, Edinburgh, 1846, (corresponding to the year 1262 of the Hegira.) (E.)

The Prophecies of Jeremiah, translated into the *Persian* Language.—8vo. (E.)

POLISH.

BIBLIA, to iest wszystko pismo Swieta starego i nowego przymielzar. The Holy Bible in the *Polish* Language.—8vo, Berlin, 1810. (E.)

This is a Protestant version.

BIBLIA, to iest, &c. The Bible, that is, all the Holy Scriptures of the New Testament. Printed from the Dantzic edition of 1632 for the use of the Polish Protestants.—8vo, Berlin, 1810. (E.)

Nowy Testament Paua Naszego Jezusa Christusa. The New Testament of our Lord Jesus Christ, translated from the Vulgate into the *Polish* Language. Published by the Russian Bible Society.—8vo, St. Petersburgh, 1815. (E.)

Biblia, to iest Ksiegi Starego i Nowego Testamenta. Bible, that is, the Books of the Old and New Testaments. From the Cracow edition of 1599. Published by the Russian Bible Society.—8vo, Moscow, 1822. (E.)

PORTUGUESE.

O Novo Testamento, isto he, o novo Concerto de Nosso Fiel Leuhor e Redemptor Jesu Christo, traduzido na lingas *Portugueza*. Impresso por Hamblin e Leyfang.—12mo, Monte do Alho, 1813. (F.)

A Protestant version, with numerous brief marginal notes. The translator's name is not given.

A Biblia Sagrada contendo O Novo e O Nelho Testamento, traduzido sur *Portuguez*, pelo Padre Joao Ferreira d'Almeida.—8vo, London, 1819. (F.)

Three copies. This is a Protestant version.

O Sancto Evangelho, segundo San Lucas e os Actos do Apostolos.—32mo, London, 1823. (F.)

O Novo Testamento Nosso Senhor e Salvador Jesus Christo, traduzido em *Indo-Portugueza*. J. S. Hughes.—12mo, London, 1826. (F.)

O Novo Testamento de Nosso Senhor Jesu Christo, traduzido em Portuguez Segundo a Vulgata, pelo Padre Antonio Pereira de Figuando. Published by the American Bible Society.—8vo, New York, 1839. (F.)

A Roman Catholic version.

O Novo Testamento, traduzido em Portuguez, pelo J. Ferreira A. d'Almeida. Printed by the American Bible Society.—8vo, New York, 1839. (F.)

O Novo Testamento, traduzido em Portuguez, pelo Antonio Pereira. Printed by the American Bible Society.—8vo, New York, 1839. (F.)

O Novo Testamento de Nosso Senhor e Redemptor Jesu Christo, traducido em Portuguez, pelo Padre Joao Ferreira A. d'Almeida. Reimpresso du Edicao de 1693. Revista e Emendatu.—32mo, Oporto, 1840. (F.)

O Novo Testamento, traducido em Portuguez pelo J. Ferreira A. d'Almeida. Printed by the American Bible Society.—8vo, New York, 1848. (F.)

PUNJABEE or SHIKH, (India.)

The New Testament, in the *Punjabee* Language.—8vo, Serampore, 1811. (E.)

THE GOSPEL according to St. Matthew, translated from the original Greek into the *Punjabee* Language, by the Lodiana Missionaries. American Mission Press.—8vo, Lodiana, 1840. Two copies. (E.)

THE GOSPEL by St. John, translated as above, with the aid of learned natives. American Presbyterian Mission Press.—8vo, Lodiana, 1841. Two copies. (E.)

THE FOUR GOSPELS and the ACTS OF THE APOSTLES, translated into the *Punjabee* Language. American Presbyterian Mission Press for the American Bible Society.—8vo, Lodiana, 1845. (E.)

THE GOSPEL according to St. Matthew, in *Punjabee.* American Presbyterian Mission Press for the American Bible Society.—12mo, Lodiana, 1845. (E.)

THE GOSPEL according to St. Mark, in *Punjabee.* American Presbyterian Mission Press for the American Bible Society.—12mo, Lodiana, 1846. (E.)

PUSHTOO or AFFGHAN, (Persia.)

THE HOLY BIBLE, containing the Old and New Testaments, translated from the originals into the *Pushtoo* Language, by the Serampore Missionaries. Vol. V., containing the New Testament. Printed at the Mission Press.—8vo, Serampore, 1818. (E.)

REVALIAN. (See Esthonian.)

ROMANESE, (Southern Europe.)

LA S. BIBLA, ner la Soinchia Scartira D'Ilg Veder Testament. Messa giu ent ilg Languaig Rumonsch da la Ligia Grischa. The Holy Scriptures of the Old Testament, translated into the *Romanese* Language from the Greek.—8vo, Coira, 1818. (E.)

Ilg Nief Testament, &c. THE NEW TESTAMENT, in *Romanese,* (Upper Dialect.)—8vo, Coira, 1820. (E.)

RUSS.

The Four Gospels, in the *Mordvinian* dialect.—8vo, St. Petersburgh, 1821. (D.)

Printed for a Finnish tribe on the banks of the Oka and Volga.

The New Testament, in Slavonic (or ancient) and modern *Russ.*—8vo, St. Petersburgh, 1822. (D.)

Printed in parallel columns.

SAMOGITIAN or LITHUANIAN, (Central Europe.)

Naujas Istatimas Jezaus Christaus Wieszpaties Musu Lietuwiszku Lezuwiu Iszquldítas par Jozapa Arnulpa Kunigaykszti Giedrayti Wiskupa Ziemayciu, Zeuklinika S. Stanislowo. Iszspanstas pas Kunigns Missionorius. The New Testament of our Lord Jesus Christ, translated into the *Samogitian* Language, &c.—4to, Wiln, 1816. (E.)

A dialect spoken near Poland. This copy is printed on blue paper.

SANSKRIT, (India.)

The Psalms of David, faithfully rendered from the original Hebrew into *Sanskrit* verse, by the Calcutta Baptist Missionaries, with native assistants. Printed at the Mission Press for the American and Foreign Bible Society.—12mo, Calcutta, 1839. (E.)

The Sanskrit is the sacred language of Hindostan.

The Four Gospels and the Acts of the Apostles, in the *Sanskrit* Language. Printed at the Baptist Mission Press for the American and Foreign Bible Society.—8vo, Calcutta, 1840. (E.)

The New Testament of our Lord and Saviour Jesus Christ, translated from the Greek into the *Sanskrit* Language, by the Calcutta Baptist Missionaries, with native assistants. Printed as above.—8vo, Calcutta, 1841. (E.)

SIAMESE, (Indo-China.)

The Gospel according to St. Matthew, in the *Siamese* Language, by J. F. Jones.—8vo. Pamphlet. (E.)

This is a second edition of 5000 copies.

The Gospel according to St. Mark, in the *Siamese* Language, by E. Robinson.—8vo. Pamphlet. (E.)

The Gospel according to St. Luke, translated into the *Siamese* Language, by Mr. Gutzlaff.—8vo. Pamphlet. (E.)

The first seven chapters of the Book of Acts, in the *Siamese* Language.—4to, 1836. Pamphlet. (E.)

The Gospel according to Mark, translated into the *Siamese* Language from the original Greek. Revised by S. Mattoon. A. M. A Press.—8vo, Bangkok, 1851. (E.)

The Gospel according to John, translated into the *Siamese* Language from the original Greek. Revised by S. Mattoon. A. M. A. Press.—8vo, Bangkok, 1851. (E.)

There is another copy of Mark and John, bound in one volume.

The Gospel according to Matthew, translated into the *Siamese* Language from the original Greek. Revised by S. Mattoon. A. M. A. Press.—8vo, Bangkok, 1853. (E.)

The Gospel according to Luke, translated into the *Siamese* Language from the original Greek. Revised by S. Mattoon. A. M. A. Press.—8vo, Bangkok, 1854. (E.)

SLAVONIC, (Wendisch.)

BIBLIA, tu ie, use Suetu Pismu Slasiga inu Noviga Ttestamenta, Slovenski, tolmazhena, Skussi. The Bible; that is, all the Holy Scriptures of the Old and New Testaments, translated into the *Slavonian* Language (Wendisch).—Fol., Wittenburgh, 1584. (D.)

The Slavonian language is spoken from the Adriatic to the North Sea, and from the Caspian to the Baltic.

Novyi Saviet Gospoda Nash ego Jisonsa Christa, &c. The New Testament of our Lord Jesus Christ, translated into the *Slavonic* Language.—8vo, St. Petersburgh. (D.)

THE HOLY BIBLE, containing the Old and New Testaments, in the *Slavonian* characters, used by the Russian Church.—8vo. (D.)

THE NEW TESTAMENT, &c., in the *Slavonian* characters, used by the Russian Church.—8vo. (D.)

BIBLIA, ili Kingi Svashennago Pisania Vetkhago i Novago Savieta. THE BIBLE; or, the Holy Scriptures of the Old and New Testaments.—8vo, St. Petersburg. (D.)

See, also, under *Russ*.

SPANISH.

See Castalio, under *Foreign Commentaries*, for a version of 1551.

La Biblia, que es, Los Sacros Libros Del Vieio y Nuevo Testamento. Trasladada en Español, por Cassiodoro de Reyna.—4to. 1622. (F.)

It has no place of publication. The initials of the translator are at the end of the Preface. On the reverse of the title page are the Decrees of the Council of Trent, from the Index of Prohibited Books, printed in Latin and Spanish. In the Preface, which is in Latin, are two wood cuts representing Ezekiel's vision and the destruction of Tyre. The work contains arguments and summaries to the books, with references and notes explanatory of the Hebrew and Greek readings. The translator is supposed to have been a Protestant, but attached the rules of the Prohibitory Index, to appear a Catholic. The Errata at the end bear date 1569. It is a very rare book, especially in good condition, as is this copy. From a curious device of the printer in the title page, representing a tree with a large hole in the trunk, in which a swarm of bees have made their honey; a mallet suspended from a branch of the tree; and a *bear*, in an erect posture, endeavouring to rob the hive, this book has been designated "The Bear Bible." At the foot of the tree lies an open book, covered with bees. [See Pettigrew's Sussexiana, p. 227-30.] From the description given in the same work (p. 232) of the edition of 1622, and from the agreement of the present copy with the above description of the edition of 1569 instead of that edition, there is a manifest discrepancy between the character of the copy and its date.

La Biblia Vulgata Latina, traducida en Espanol y Anotada conforme al sentido de los Santos Padres y expositores catolicos, por el P. Phelipe Scio de S. Miguel, de las escuelas pias, &c. Segunda edicion.—19 vols. 8vo, Madrid, 1794-97. (F.)

The first edition of this (Scio's) Spanish version of the Vulgate was in ten volumes, folio. In this edition the Old Testament is in fifteen volumes, and the New Testament in four. The text is in double columns, and the notes, which are principally from the ancient Fathers, are arranged below the text.

El Nuevo Testamento de Nuestro Senor Jesu Christo.—12mo, Bermondsey, 1813. (F.)

A Protestant version.

El Nuevo Testamento de Nuestro Senor y Redentor Jesu Cristo. Nueva Edicion, cui dadosamente corregida.—12mo, 1817. (F.)

A Protestant version. It is without the place of publication.

El Nuevo Testamento, (Scio,) reimpreso a la segunda edicion en Madrid 1797. Printed by the American Bible Society.—12mo, New York, 1819. Two copies. (F.)

La Biblia, o' el Antiguo y Nuevo Testamento, traducidos al Español, de la Vulgata Latina, por el R. P. Phelipe Scio de S. Miguel.—8vo, London, 1821. (F.)

There are two copies of this edition, one of which is defective, the title page and nearly all of the first two books of the Old Testament being wanting.

El Nuevo Testamento, (Scio,) reimpreso a la segunda edicion en Madrid 1797. Printed by the American Bible Society.—12mo, New York, 1822. (F.)

Los libros Sagrados de los Psalmos de los Proverbios, del Ecclesiastes, y de la Prophecia de Isaias; traducidos al Español de la Vulgata Latina, por el R. P. Phelipe Scio de S. Miguel.—32mo, Paris, 1823. (F.)

Biblia Sagrada, &c., translated by Scio from the Vulgate into Spanish.—8vo, New York, 1824. (F.)

El Nuevo Testamento; Nuevomente traducido de la Vulgata Latina al Español, alcarado el sentido Algunos lugares con la luz que dan los testos originales Hebrèo y Griego, por Don Felix Tovies Amat. Edicion revista, Formada Sobre lague le imprimió en Madrid Año de 1823.—12mo, London, 1825. (F.)

La Biblia Sagrada, en Espanol, &c.—8vo, New York, 1826. (F.)

La Biblia Vulgata Latina, traducida en Espanol, y annotada conforme al sentido des los Santos Padres, y expositores Catolicos, por Don Felipe Scio de San Miguel. Primera Edicion Megicana, Sacada de la tercera y ultima de España.—20 vols. 4to, Mexico, 1831-5. (F.)

This edition contains the Vulgate Latin text, as well as Scio's translation. It has the same preliminary matter as the octavo Madrid edition, with the same chronological Tables and Indexes appended.

El Nuevo Testamento, (Scio,) reimpreso a la segunda edicion en Madrid 1797. Printed by the American Bible Society.—12mo, New York, 1831. (F.)

El Nuevo Testamento, traducido al Castellano por Cipriano de Valera en 1602 y revisada en 1831, &c.—12mo, London, 1832. (F.)

Two copies. This is a Protestant version.

La Biblia Sagrada, en Espanol, &c.—8vo, New York, 1832. (F.)

La Biblia Sagrada, traducidos de la Vulgata Latina en Español, (Scio.)—8vo, New York, 1832. (E.)

El Nuevo Testamento, traducido al Espanol de la Vulgata Latina, por el R. P. Phelipe Scio de San Miguel.—12mo, Paris, 1836. (F.)

El Nuevo Testamento, traducido al Espanol, (Scio.) Published by the American Bible Society.—18mo, New York, 1837. (F.)

A Roman Catholic version.

El Nuevo Testamento de Nuestro Senor Jesu-Christo, traducido de la Vulgata Latina al Español, por Don Felix Torres Amat.

Nueva Edicion, Corregida y revisada por la Sociedad para promover al conocimiento Cristiano.—8vo, London, 1837. (F.)

This is a Romish version of the Spanish Testament, and said to be superior to Scio's translation.

El Santo Evangelio de Jesu Christo segun San Lucas, &c. The Gospel according to St. Luke, translated from the Latin into Spanish.—18mo, Madrid, 1837. (F.)

Los cuatro Evangelios; traducidos del Griego al Español, é illustrados con notas, por Don Guillermo Harris Bub, presbiterio de la Iglesia protestante Metodista, y Superintendente de su Mission en España.—4to, Gibraltar, 1841. (F.)

A Protestant version of the four Gospels.

El Nuevo Testamento, traducido al Castellano por Cipriano de Valera en 1602. Printed by the American Bible Society.—12mo, New York, 1845. (F.)

El Nuevo Testamento de Nuestro Senor Jesu Cristo, &c.—8vo, London, 1847. (F.)

A Protestant version, revised under the direction of the Society for promoting Christian Knowledge.

La Biblia Sagrada, traducida en Espanol version, cotegada cuida dosamente con les Lenguas Antiquas.—8vo, New York, 1852. (F.)

Escrituras del Nuevo Pacto Mateo, traducion del original Griego; obra publicada por la Union Biblica Americana.—32mo, New York, 1853. (F.)

A Spanish Baptist version of the Gospel by St. Matthew.

SWEDISH.

Biblia; Thet ar all then Skrift, &c. The Holy Scriptures of the Old and New Testaments, with the Apocrypha; translated into the *Swedish* Language.—8vo, Stockholm, 1715. (E.)

Gamla Testamentet, och, Nya Testamentet. The Old and New Testaments. Published under the Superintendence of the Evangelical Society.—8vo, Stockholm, 1812. (E.)

Bibeben, eller, Then Heliga Skrift, innehallande Gamla och Nya Testamentet. The Bible, or, the Holy Scriptures, containing the canonical books of the Old and New Testaments; according to the octavo edition of the Swedish Bible Society. Published by the British and Foreign Bible Society.—8vo, London, 1828. (E.)

Gamla Testamentet, och, Nya Testamentet. The Old Testament (22d edition) and the New Testament (34th edition). Published by the Swedish Bible Society.—8vo, Stockholm, 1845. Two copies. (E.)

NYA TESTAMENTET, &c. The New Testament, in the *Swedish* Language. Printed for the Swedish Bible Society.—8vo, Stockholm, 1846. (E.)

SYRIAC.

Novum Domini Nostri Jesu Christi Testamentum Syriace; cum omnibus Vocalibus et Versione Latinâ Matthaei ita adornatâ, ut unico hoc Evangelista intellecto, reliqui totius operis libri, sine interprete facile intelligi possint, &c. Accurante Aegidio Gutbirio, S.T.D., &c.—12mo, Hamburg, 1664. (H.)

This is the second edition of the Syriac New Testament, (Gutbirius,) with the Latin version of the Gospel of St. Matthew at the bottom of the pages.

NOVUM TESTAMENTUM Syriacum; cum versione Latina; cura et studio Johannis Leusden et Caroli Schaaf, editum; ad omnes editiones diligenter recensitum; et Variis Lectionibus, magno labore collectis, adornatum. Secunda Editio, a mendis purgata.—4to, Lugduni Batav., 1717. (H.)

This, according to Michaelis, is the *Editio Princeps* of the Syriac New Testament. This copy has not the Lexicon which usually accompanies this edition.

NOVUM TESTAMENTUM Syriaco, denuo recognitum atque ad Fidem codicum Manuscriptorum emendatum, &c.—4to, London, 1816. (H.)

PSALTERIUM SYRIACE. The Book of Psalms, in Syriac. Published by the Bible Society.—8vo, London, 1825. (H.)

VETUS ET NOVUM TESTAMENTUM, in ancient and modern Syriac, in parallel columns; the former being the Peschito version, and the latter a translation from the original Hebrew. Printed for the American Board of Commissioners of Foreign Missions at the expense of the American Bible Society.—4to, Ooroomiah. (E.)

The modern Syriac is the vernacular language of the Nestorians. This translation was made by the missionaries, who reduced the language to writing. It has no date of publication.

The Epistle of Paul to the Galatians, in modern Syriac. Printed at the expense of the American Bible Society by the American Board of Commissioners of Foreign Missions.—8vo, Ooroomiah. Pamphlet. Two copies. (H.)

SYRO-CHALDAIC.

The Four Gospels, in the *Syro-Chaldaic* Language, with the *Nestorian* character.—4to, London, 1829. (H.)

TAHEITAN.

The Gospel according to St. Luke, translated into the *Otaheitan* Language by the missionaries of the London Missionary Society.—12mo, Eimeo, 1820. Two copies. (E.)

Tae Evanelia a Mataio, no Jesu Christ to Tatou Fatu; Iriti lua i Paru Tahiti; The Gospel according to St. Matthew, in the *Taheitan* Language. Printed at the Windward Mission Press.—12mo, Tahiti, 1820. (E.)

The volume also contains the Gospel by St. John.

The Acts of the Apostles, in the *Otaheitan* Language. Printed at the Leeward Mission Press.—12mo, Tahaa, 1823. (E.)

The Gospel according to St. John; the Book of Acts; Paul's Epistles to the Galatians, Ephesians, Colossians, Thessalonians, and to Timothy, Titus, and Philemon; in the *Taheitan* Language. Printed at the Mission Press.—12mo, 1824. (E.)

The Gospel by St. John; the Book of the Acts; and the Epistles, including Philemon; in the *Taheitan* Language. Printed at the Leeward Mission Press.—12mo, Tahaa, 1825. (E.)

The Gospel by John was printed at the Mission Press at Huahine, and is in a different type from the rest of the book. The volume has no general title page.

TAMUL, (Southern India.)

The Acts of the Apostles, in *Tamul* and *English*. Printed at the Church Mission Press for the Madras Auxiliary Bible Society.—12mo, Madras, 1837. (E.)

Paul's Epistles to Timothy, in the *Tamul* Language. Published by the Jaffna Auxiliary Bible Society.—64mo, 1837. (E.)

The Holy Scriptures of the Old Testament, in the *Tamul* Language. Printed at the American Mission Press.—8vo, Madras, 1839. (E.)

THE BOOK OF GENESIS, in the *Tamul* Language. Printed at the American Mission Press for the Jaffna Auxiliary Bible Society.—18mo, 1839. (E.)

THE NEW TESTAMENT of our Lord and Saviour Jesus Christ, in the *Tamul* Language. Printed at the American Mission Press for the Madras Auxiliary Bible Society.—8vo, Madras, 1840. (E.)

Selections from the Holy Scriptures, containing Genesis, Exodus, Psalms, Luke, Acts, Romans, and First and Second Epistles of John, in the *Tamul* Language. Printed for the Madras Auxiliary Bible Society at the American Mission Press.—12mo, Madras, 1840. (E.)

The Gospel by St. Luke and the Acts of the Apostles, in *Tamul.* American Mission Press for the American Madras Mission.—18mo, Madras, 1841. Four copies. (E.)

THE HOLY BIBLE, translated into the *Tamul* Language. The Old Testament from the original, by the Rev. J. P. Fabricius; the New Testament by the Rev. C. T. E. Rhenius. Revised by the Committee of the Madras Auxiliary Bible Society, &c. Printed for that and the American Bible Society at the American Mission Press.—8vo, Madras, 1844. (E.)

THE NEW TESTAMENT, &c., in the *Tamul* Language. Printed as above.—8vo, Madras, 1844. (E.)

This volume, bound in calf and marbled, is the work of native mechanics.

THE GOSPEL by St. Matthew, in the *Tamul* Language. American Mission Press for the Mission.—32mo, Madras, 1847. (E.)

THE GOSPEL by St. Mark, in *Tamul.* Sine anno.—18mo. Three copies. (E.)

THE HOLY BIBLE, in the *Tamul* Language, translated under the auspices of the British and Foreign Bible Society.—4to, Madras, 1850. (E.)

THE HOLY BIBLE, &c., in the *Tamul* Language. Printed at the American Mission Press.—8vo, Madras, 1850. (E.)

TARTAR.

THE NEW TESTAMENT, &c., in the *Orenburgh* Tartar Dialect.—8vo, Astrachan, 1820. Two copies. (E.)

TSCHEREMISSIAN, (Russia.)

Mia Ospod'nan Jisus Cristosan Sviatoi Evangel'ia. The Four Gospels, translated into the *Tscheremissian* Dialect.—8vo, St. Petersburgh, 1821. (E.)

This dialect is spoken in the eastern part of Siberia. This version is for a Finnish tribe on the banks of the Volga and Kama, in the governments of Kasan and Simbersk.

TELINGA, (Southern India.)

The Holy Bible, containing the Old and New Testaments, translated from the originals into the *Telinga* Language, by the Serampore Missionaries. Vol. V., containing the New Testament. Printed at the Mission Press.—8vo, Serampore, 1818. (E.)

TURKISH.

The New Testament of our Lord and Saviour Jesus Christ, translated into the *Turkish* Language. Sine loco.—8vo, 1814. (D.)

The New Testament, &c., *Turco-Greek*.—8vo, Constantinople, 1826. (D.)

The Holy Bible, or, the Old and New Testaments, in the *Turkish* Language. Hali Bey's edition, by Prof. Keiffer.—4to, Paris, 1827. (D.)

See *Graeco-Turkish*.

VAUDOIS. (See French.)

VIKANERA or BIKANEERA, (Central India.)

The Holy Bible, containing the Old and New Testaments, translated from the originals into the *Vikanera* Language, by the Serampore Missionaries. Vol. V., containing the New Testament. Printed at the Mission Press.—8vo, Serampore, 1820. (E.)

WELSH.

Y Bibl Cyssegr-Lan, sef, yr Hen Destament a'r Newydd. The Holy Bible; or, the Old and New Testaments.—8vo, London, 1717. (E.)

It is preceded by a Liturgy, and followed by the Psalms of David in metre.

Y Bibl Cyssegr-Lan, sef, yr Hen Destament a'r Newydd, &c.—8vo, London, 1804. (E.)

Y Bibl Cyssegr-Lan, &c. The Holy Bible; or, the Old and New Testaments, in the *Welsh* Language.—12mo, Caer Grawnt, 1813. Two copies. (E.)

Y Bibl Cyssegr-Lan, sef, yr Hen Destament a'r Newydd. Printed for the British and Foreign Bible Society.—8vo, London, 1814. Two copies. (E.)

Testament Newydd, ein Harglwydd a'n Hiachawdwr Iesu Grist. The New Testament of our Lord and Saviour Jesus Christ, in the *Welsh* Language. Printed for the British and Foreign Bible Society.—8vo, London, 1829. (E.)

Y Bibl Cyssegr-Lan, &c. The Holy Bible, in the *Welsh* Language.—12mo, Caer Grawnt, 1831. (E.)

Testament Newydd, &c. The New Testament, in the *Welsh* Language.—12mo, London, 1831. (E.)

Testament Newydd, ein Harglwydd a'n Hiachawdwr Iesu Grist. The New Testament, in *Welsh* and *English*. Printed by G. E. Eyre and W. Spottiswoode for the British and Foreign Bible Society.— Ruby 32mo, London, 1853. (E.)

WENDISH. (See Slavonic.)

MANUSCRIPTS.

Liber Esther Hebraice. MS. Saec. 23. (D.)

This is a rolled manuscript, and measures 7 feet 2 inches. The Sections are 3½ by 3 inches. It is written on vellum in small Hebrew characters, and without points or any ornament whatever. The author and date are unknown.

The Four Gospels in *Syriac*. Written in the ancient Estrangelo character; arranged in lessons for the Liturgy of the Jacobite Syrian Church. No date.—Fol. (D.)

The age of this manuscript is not known, though it is obviously of great antiquity. It was given to Dr. Grant, Missionary to the Nestorians, by a Syrian priest at Mosul, and by him presented to the American Bible Society. It is written on paper in a large, bold character, and is very regularly executed.

The Holy Scriptures of the Old Testament, translated into the *Turkish* Language with the Armenian character, for the use of Armenians who speak principally the Turkish.—4 vols. 4to. (D.)

This is the original translation of the Old Testament into Armeno-Turkish, made under the direction of Rev. Mr. Goodell, (a missionary of the American Board of Commissioners of Foreign Missions at Constantinople,) by Dionysius Carabet, an Armenian bishop. It was made at Malta, and afterwards revised by Mr. Goodell and Mr. Pariotes at Constantinople. It was printed at Smyrna at the expense of the American Bible Society.

The Pentateuch; or, Five Books of Moses, in *Armenian* MS., on paper.—4to. (D.)

A Manuscript translation of the Scriptures into the English language, made by some former member of Princeton College, N. J.—Fol. (G.)

An ancient oriental Manuscript, written on vellum. Unknown.—4to. (D.)

ENGLISH COMMENTARIES.

CALVIN, JOHN.—A Commentary on the Epistle to the Romans. Translated by F. Libson.—12mo, Philadelphia, 1836. (C.)

CALVIN, JOHN.—A Commentary on the Psalms of David. —3 vols. 8vo, Oxford, 1840. (C.)

CAMPBELL, GEORGE, D.D.—The Four Gospels, translated from the Greek, &c.; with Notes critical and explanatory.—2 vols. 8vo, London, 1834. (C.)

CARYL, JOSEPH.—An Exposition of the Book of Job.—4to, 1659. (C.)

CHEKE, SIR JOHN.—The Gospel by St. Matthew, and part of the first chapter of St. Mark, translated into English from the Greek, with Notes.—8vo, Cambridge and London, 1843. (C.)

CLARK, SAMUEL.—A Family Bible, with Annotations, parallel Texts, &c.—4to, London, 1760. (C.)

This work was first published in 1690. The author acknowledges that he has sometimes incorporated the marginal readings into the text, and changed the Italic words. This copy has a Preface by George Whitfield.

CLARKE, ADAM, LL.D.—The Holy Bible, &c., including marginal Readings and parallel Texts, with a Commentary, &c.—6 vols. 4to, New York, 1811. (C.)

CLARKE, ADAM, LL.D.—The Holy Bible, &c., as above.— 6 vols. 4to, New York, 1825. (C.)

CORAY.—A Commentary on the Epistles to Timothy and Titus.—8vo, 1835. (C.)

FRANK, AUGUSTUS HERMAN.—A Guide to the reading and study of the Holy Scriptures, with an illustrative Supplement.—8vo, London, 1803. (C.)

FULKE, WILLIAM.—The New Testament, and Annotations of the Rhemish Translators, [from the Latin Vulgate,] with the Translation of the Church of England, in parallel columns, with Answers to the Annotations. —Fol., London, about 1600. (C.)

The title page is wanting.

FULKE, WILLIAM.—A Relic of the original Edition of Fulke's Confutation of the Rhemish Annotations to the New Testament.—Fol., London, about 1600. (C.)

This copy contains his "Defence of the English Translation of the Bible" entire, except the title page.

GEDDES, REV. ALEXANDER, LL.D.—Prospectus of a new Translation of the Holy Bible, &c., with various Readings, explanatory Notes, and critical Observations, &c.—4to, Glasgow, 1786. (C.)

HAAK, THEODORE, ESQ.—The Dutch Annotations upon the New Testament, &c., with the authorized Translation of all the Text; now faithfully communicated to the use of Great Britain in English.—Fol., London, 1657. (C.)

This copy is deficient in the title page and contents to the 16th chapter of Matthew.

HAWEIS, REV. THOMAS, LL.D.—The Evangelical Expositor; or, a Commentary on the Holy Bible, &c.—Fol. The Old Testament printed at Edinburgh, 1817; the New Testament at London, 1821. (C.)

This work is in English type, with the commentary interspersed, and numerous engravings, and is a very fine edition of the Bible. The vignette is a fanciful attempt to describe the appearance of the earth in its different stages of creation.

HENRY, MATTHEW.—An Exposition of the Old and New Testaments, with practical Remarks, &c. Seventh edition.—3 vols. fol., Edinburgh, 1767-69. (C.)

HENRY, MATTHEW.—Another copy of the above, edited by Burder and Hughes, with the Life of the Author.—6 vols. 8vo, Philadelphia, 1828. (C.)

This is the first American edition, with a Preface by Dr. A. Alexander.

HORNE, THOMAS HARTWELL.—Introduction to the Critical Study of the Holy Scriptures.—4 vols. 8vo, Philadelphia, 1831. (C.)

HORNE, THOMAS HARTWELL.—Another copy of the above, from the seventh London edition.—2 vols. 8vo, Philadelphia, 1835-6. (C.)

HUTCHESON, GEORGE.—A brief Exposition of the Twelve small Prophets, &c.—Fol., London, 1657. (C.)

MACKNIGHT, JAMES, D.D.—A new and literal Translation from the original, of the Apostle Paul's first and second Epistles to the Thessalonians, with a Commentary, &c.—4to, London, 1787. (C.)

MACKNIGHT, JAMES, D.D.—A new literal Translation, &c., of all the Apostolical Epistles, with a Commentary, &c.; to which is added a History of the Apostle's Life.—8vo, London, 1835. (C.)

MAYER, JOHN.—A Commentary upon the New Testament, representing the divers Expositions thereof, &c., by ancient and modern Writers; and hereby sifting out the true Sense of every Passage, &c. Vol. II., (imperfect.)—Fol., London, 1631. (C.)

PERRIN, REV. W.—Hebrew Canticles; or, a poetical Commentary or Paraphrase on the various Songs of Scripture, &c.—18mo, Philadelphia, 1820. (C.)

RAY, J. M.—A revised Translation and Interpretation of the Sacred Scriptures, after the Eastern manner, from concurrent Authorities, &c., showing that the inspired Writings contain the Seeds of the valuable Sciences, &c., and the connexion of Natural Science with Revealed Religion. —4to, Glasgow, 1815. (C.)

SCOTT, THOMAS.—The Holy Bible, &c., with original Notes, practical Observations, and copious References. Improved edition.— 6 vols. 8vo, New York, 1810. (C.)

TURNER, SAMUEL H., D.D.—A Companion to the Book of Genesis.—8vo, New York and London, 1841. (C.)

COMMENTARIES

IN FOREIGN LANGUAGES.

BALDWIN. See SCHMID.

CALVIN, JOHN.—In omnes Pauli Apostoli Epistolas, atque etia in Epistolam ad Hebraeos, Jo. Calvini Commentarii, &c. Etiam, Joannis Calvini Commentarii in Epistolas Canonicas, Petri, Joannis, Jacobi et Judae, &c.—2 vols. in 1, fol., Geneva, 1554-57. (C.)

This edition was printed under the inspection of the author. This copy belonged to the Library of an Independent minister in London, who received it, by a succession of bequests, from a refugee to Geneva during the reign of the bloody Mary, and who returned to England after the accession of Elizabeth.

CALVIN, JOHN.—Commentaires de Jean Calvin, sur les cinq livres de Moyse; or, the Commentaries of John Calvin, (in French,) on the Book of Genesis, with a Harmony of the other four Books of the Pentateuch. —Fol., Geneva, 1564. (C.)

This edition has a curious and rather mysterious vignette on the title page.

CARRIER, PERE.—Le Nouveau Testament de notre Seigneur Jesus Christ, traduit en Francaise, avec le Commentaire literal du Pere Carrieres dans le Texte, et des Notes explicative, morales et dogmatique, pour en faciliter l'intelligence, &c.—8vo, Quebec, 1846. (C.)

This is a Roman Catholic version from the Vulgate, with a Commentary.

CASTALIA, SEBASTIAN.—Biblia interprete Sebastiano Castalione una cum ejusdem Annotationibus.—Fol., Basil, 1551. (F.)

"This is a copy of the first edition of this version. It is printed in Italic type, and is said to be the first Bible so printed. The annotations are at the end of the work, in Roman type. Castalia was employed eight years on this version of the Bible. His object was to translate the Scriptures into elegant Latin, like that of the ancient classics. He has been censured by some, and vindicated by others, particularly by Professor Dathe and Dr. Campbell." [Lowndes' Librarian, p. 37.]

CHRYSOSTOM, ST.—A Commentary on the Epistle to the Galatians, in Modern Greek.—Malta, 1833. (C.)

DEAN, W.—The Book of Exodus in Chinese, with Notes. —8vo, Hongkong, 1851. Pamphlet. (D.)

DATHE, JOANNES AUGUSTUS.—Psalterium Syriacum recesuit et Latine vertit Thomas Erpenius, Notas philologicas et criticas addidit Joannes Augustus Dathe.—8vo, Halle, 1768. (H.)

ERPENIUS. See DATHE, JOANNES AUGUSTUS.

HARE, FRANCIS.—Psalmorum Liber, in versiculos metrice divisus, &c., cum dissertatione de antiqua Hebraeorum Poesi, aliisque quaesitis ad Psalmorum Librum pertinentibus, &c.—2 vols. 8vo, London, 1736. (C.)

JARCHI, SOLOMON.—The Pentateuch in Hebrew, with the Commentary of Solomon Jarchi; with the Books of Canticles, Ruth, Lamentations, Ecclesiastes, and Esther, and the Kaphtoroth, or Lessons for the Sabbaths and Festivals, with Masoretic Notes. Second edition.—4to, Venice, A. M. 5367—A.D. 1607. (H.)

LAMPE, FREDERIC ADOLPH.—Uitlegging van het Evangelie van den H. Johannes, &c.; or, A Commentary on the Gospel of St. John, translated into Dutch from the Latin of Frederic Adolph Lampe, Professor, &c., at Utrecht. Written in 1723.—4to, Rotterdam, (Date gone.) Imperfect. (C.)

LAPIDE.—R. P. C. Cornelii a Lapide e Societate Jesu, Sacrae Scripturae, olim Lovanii, postea Romae, Prof. Commentaria in S. Scripturam. Editio novissima anterioribus auctior et correctior, ac Indicibus necessariis illustrata.—10 vols. fol., Venice, 1761. (B.)

"This is the work of a learned French Jesuit, and is, by some critics, regarded as a chef d'oeuvre of erudition. He wrote on the entire Bible, except the Books of Job and Psalms. It contains a great mass of learning, mixed up with legends, fables, and many weak and foolish things." [Lowndes' British Librarian, p. 115.]

LOWRIE, W. M.—A Commentary on the Gospel by Luke, in the Chinese Language.—8vo. Pamphlet. (D.)

MOLLER, D. HENRICI.—Enarrationis Psalmorum Davidis, ex praelectionibus D. Henrici Molleri, Hambergensis. Novissima Editio, prioribus emendatior.—Fol., Geneva, 1619. (C.)

"The author was a Calvinist, and an eminent Hebraist, and the work is said to be a judicious explication."

MUTHESIUS, ZACHARIAH.—Novi Testamenti versionis Vulgatae, correctae, ad Normani Libri Concordiae, cum additionibus locorum communium paraphrasticis, et explicatione locorum controversorum genuina, &c.—4to, Frankfort, 1611. (H.)

This work is in two parts; the first containing the four Evangelists and the Acts of the Apostles; the second, the Epistles and the Apocalypse. The commentary, which is very full and runs through the work, is thus stated in the title: Filo Dnn. Hunnii, Mylii, Rungii, Brentii, Chemnith: tum, si qua opus fuit veraedoctrinae hostium, deducta et agglomerata.

PISCATOR, JOHN.—Analysis Logica Epistolae Pauli ad Romanos; una cum Scholiis et observationibus locorum doctrinae Authore Johan Piscatore, Prof., &c. Fourth edition.—12mo, Herborn, (Nassau,) 1668. (C.)

PRADUS. See VILLALPANDUS.

SCHARPIO, D. M. JOANNE.—Symphonia Prophetarum et Apostolorum, in qua ordine chronologico loci Sacrae Scripturae specietenus contradicentes, conciliantur.—4to, Geneva, 1625. (C.)

SCHMID, JOSEPH.—Josephi Schmidii in Prophetas minores Commentarius, cum D. Frederici Balduini, intres posteriores Prophetas Commentario. Second edition.—4to, Leipsic, 1698. (C.)

SCIO. See *Holy Scriptures in Foreign Languages.*

VATABLE, FRANCIS.—Biblia Sacra cum universis Franc. Vatabli, &c., et variorum Interpretum Annotationibus. Latina interpretatio duplex est; altera Vetus altera Nova, &c.—2 vols. fol., Paris, 1729 and 1745. (C.)

This Bible is printed in two columns; the inner one is the version of Sanctis Pagninus; the outer, the Vulgate, &c.

VILLALPANDUS.—Hieronymi Pradi et Joannis Baptistae Villalpandi e Societate Jesu, in Ezechielem Explanationes, et Apparatus urbis ac Temple Hierosolymitani, Commentariis et imaginibus illustratus, opus tribus Tomis distinctum.—3 vols. fol., Rome, 1596-1604. (C.)

'A work displaying great research, learning, and industry. Copies are seldom found in good condition, particularly as to the plates." [Lowndes.] This copy is a very fine one in every respect.

ANONYMOUS.

Critici Sacri; sive Annotata Doctissimorum Virorum in V. ac N. Testamentum; quibus accedunt Tractatus varii Theologico-philologici.—7 vols. fol., Frankfort on the Mayne, 1695. (C.)

This collection of Biblical critics was first published in London A.D. 1660, and designed as a companion to Walton's Polyglott Bible. Some of the most celebrated critics, whose dissertations and comments on the Scriptures are found in this work, are Vatable, Castalius, Hugo Grotius, Joseph Scaliger, Arius Montanus, Sebastian Munster, Erasmus, Casaubon, Archbishop Usher, Henry Stephens, &c.

The Pentateuch in Hebrew, with a Rabbinical Commentary in Hebrew Spanish.—2 vols. 4to. Two copies. (H.)

The First volume of another copy.—4to. (H.)

A Paraphrase and Scholia on Paul's Epistles to Timothy and Titus, &c., in Greek.—4to, Malta, 1829. (C.)

The Acts of the Apostles in Modern Greek, with Notes, Philological, Historical, Dogmatical, and Ethical.—8vo, Malta, 1827. (H.)

Synoptical View of the Parables of the New Testament, translated from English into Modern Greek.—12mo, Malta, 1835. (H.)

The Book of the Five Parts of the Law, or the Pentateuch, in Hebrew, with a Rabbinical Commentary in Hebrew Spanish. In two Parts. Printed for the British and Foreign Bible Society.—2 vols. 8vo, Bonn. (No date.) (H.)

The Book of the Holy Writings of the Law, the Prophets, and the Psalms, with a Hebrew Spanish Rabbinical Commentary. Printed for the British and Foreign Bible Society.—2 vols. 4to, Bonn. (No date.) (H.)

The Book of the Holy Writings of the Law, &c., containing the Pentateuch, with the Song of Solomon, Ruth, Lamentations, Ecclesiastes, and Esther. First Part. Printed for the British and Foreign Bible Society.—4to, Bonn. (No date.) (H.)

GRAMMATICAL WORKS.

AUCHER, PASCHAL, D.D.—Grammar, English and Armenian.—12mo, Venice, 1817. (C.)

BARNARD, SAMUEL.—A Polyglott Grammar of the Hebrew, Chaldee, Syriac, Greek, Latin, English, French, Italian, Spanish, and German Languages, reduced to one common Rule of Syntax, and a uniform Mode of Declension and Conjugation, as far as practicable, &c., &c.—8vo, Philadelphia, 1825. (C.)

BELCOURT, G. A.—Principes de la Langue des Sauvages. Appeles Sauteux.—12mo, Quebec, 1839. (C.)

CHAMBAUD, LEWIS.—A Grammar of the French Tongue. —12mo, London, 1812. (C.)

CURAS, H.—A Grammar of the French Language, in German.—8vo, Berlin, 1756. (C.)

DAKOTA.—A Grammar and Dictionary of the Dakota Language, collected by the Members of the Dakota Mission, &c.—4to, Washington, D. C., 1832. (C.)

DELPINO, JOSEPH.—Elements of the Spanish Language, &c., &c.; to which is added, an English Grammar for Spaniards.—8vo, London, 1814. (C.)

A standard Spanish Grammar.

DE SACY, A. I. SILVESTRE.—Grammaire Arabe a l'usage des Eleves de l'ecole Speciale des Langues orientales vivantes, &c.—8vo, Paris, 1810. (C.)

DWIGHT, H. G. O.—The English and Armenian Grammar.—8vo, Smyrna, 1835. (C.)

GILCHRIST, JAMES.—Philosophic Etymology, or Rational Grammar.—8vo, London, 1816. (C.)

GREEN, REV. THOMAS SHELDON, M.A.—A Treatise on the Grammar of the New Testament Dialect, &c., &c.—8vo, London, 1842. (C.)

JONES, SIR WILLIAM.—A Grammar of the Persian Language, with Specimens of Arabic and Persian Handwriting, &c.—4to, London, 1828. (C.)

LOBATO, &c.—A Portuguese and English Grammar, compiled from those of Lobato, Durham Lane, and Wieyra, &c., by a Professor of the Spanish and Portuguese Languages in St. Mary's College.—12mo, Baltimore, 1820. Two copies. (C.)

LOEILLOT, M.—Nouveau Elemens de Grammaire Russe, &c., ou correspondence entre deux amis qui etudient la langue Russe.—8vo, St. Petersburgh, 1812. (C.)

LUDOLF, JOB.—Grammatica Aethopica; Ab ipso Autre solicite revisa, et plurimis in locis correcta et aucta. Second edition.—Fol., Frankfort on the Mayne, 1702. (C.)

MORRISON, REV. ROBERT.—A Grammar of the Chinese Language. Printed at the Mission Press.—4to, Serampore, 1815. (C.)

HENDERSON, ALEXANDER.—A Grammar of the Moskito Language, (Balize, Honduras.)—8vo, New York, 1846. (C.)

NEGRIS, ALEXANDER.—A Grammar of the Modern Greek Language, with an Appendix, containing original Specimens of Prose and Verse.—12mo, Boston, 1828. (C.)

NEILSON, REV. WILLIAM, D.D.—An Introduction to the Irish Language, in three Parts, &c., with copious Tables of Contractions.—8vo, Dublin, 1808. (C.)

NEW ZEALAND.—A Grammar and Vocabulary of the Language of New Zealand, by the Church Missionary Society.—12mo, London, 1820. (C.)

PALERMO, EVANGELISTA.—A Grammar of the Italian Language, with Explanations of Terms, Rules for Pronunciation, &c., &c. Third edition.—8vo, London, 1787. (C.)

RASK, ERASMUS.—A Grammar of the Danish Language, for the use of Englishmen, &c., &c.—12mo, Copenhagen, 1830. (C.)

SUSOO.—A Grammar and Vocabulary of the Susoo Language, with the Names of some of the Susoo Towns near the Banks of the Rio Pongas, &c.—8vo, Edinburgh, 1802. (C.)

WALKER, JOHN.—A Rhetorical Grammar.—8vo, Boston, 1822. (C.)

WARNER, J. W.—A Grammar of the German Language. —18mo, New York, 1850. (C.)

WINER, DR. GEORGE BENEDICT.—A Grammar of the Idioms of the Greek Language of the New Testament. Translated by Agnew and Ebbeke.—8vo, New York, 1850. (C.)

DICTIONARIES AND LEXICONS.

ADAM, REV. M. T.—A Dictionary of the Hindee Language.—8vo, Calcutta, 1829. (C.)

AUCHER, P. PASCHAL.—Dictionnaire abrege Francais-Armenian, et Armenian-Francais.—2 vols. 8vo, Venice, 1817. (C.)

BROCKHAUS, F. A.—Dictionnaire Francais, Allemand, Anglais; ouvrage complet, redige sur un plan entierement nouveau, a l'usage des trois nations. Second edition.—8vo, Leipsic, 1836. (C.)

BUXTORF, JOHN.—Lexicon Hebraicum et Chaldaicum; complectens voces omnimodas quae in sacris Bibliis exstant, &c., &c. Accesserunt Lexicon breve Rabbinico-Philosophicum et Index Latinus.—8vo, Glasgow, 1824. (C.)

CASTELL, EDMUND, S.T.D.—Lexicon Syriacum ex ejus Lexico Heptaglotto seorsim typis describi, curavit, atque sua annotata adjecit Joannis David Michaelis.—4to, Gottingen, 1788. (C.)

CASTELL, EDMUND, S.T.D., &c.—Lexicon Heptaglotton, Hebraicum, Chaldaicum, Syriacum, Samaritanum, Aethiopicum, Arabicum, conjunctim; et Persicum, separatim. In quo omnes voces Hebraeae, Chaldaeae, Syrae, Samaritanae, Aethiopicae, Arabicae, et Persicae, tam in MSS. quam impressis libris, cumprimis autem in Bibliis Polyglottis, adjectis hinc inde Armeniis, Turcicis, Indis, Japonicis, &c., ordine alphabetico, sub singulis radicibus digestae, continentur, &c., &c., cui accessit Brevis et Harmonica Grammaticae omnium praecedentium, Linguarum Delineatio.—2 vols. fol., London, 1669. (C.)

"It is said that Dr. Castell and his assistants were employed seventeen years in the composition of this work. He spent twenty years in the public service; above £12,000 of his own estate; and for a reward, was left, at the close of the work, over £1,800 in debt. This forced him to make his condition known to the king, (Charles II., to whom the work is dedicated,) of whom he petitioned that *a jail* might not be his reward for so much service and expense." "Charles wrote to the bishops and noblemen of the realm, recommending Castell and his work *to their pity* and protection; the bishops and noblemen, in their turn, recommended the author *to the public;* and thus, between the king, his court, and the public, Dr. Castell never received a farthing." "He maintained in his own house, and at his own expense, seven Englishmen and seven foreigners, as writers, all of whom died before the work was completed. In allusion to this, he says, 'I had once companions in my undertaking, but some of them are now no more, and others have abandoned me, alarmed at the immensity of the work. I am now, therefore, left alone, without amanuensis or corrector; far advanced in years; with my patrimony exhausted, my bodily and mental strength impaired, and my eyesight almost gone.' Such were the melancholy circumstances under which the Lexicon of Castell was composed." [Dibdin.] This work generally accompanies the London (or Walton's) Polyglott, and from the Preface to the latter work, seems to have been regarded as a supplement to it.

COCCIUS, JOHANNIS.—Lexicon et Commentarius Sermonis Hebraici et Chaldaici. Opera atque studio Johannis Henrici Maji.—Fol., Frankfort and Leipsic, 1714. (C.)

DAKOTA.—Dictionary, &c. (See *Grammatical Works.*)

DONNEGAN, JAMES, M.D.—A new Greek and English Lexicon, principally on the plan of the Greek and German Lexicon of Schneider. First American edition.—8vo, Boston and New York, 1835. (C.)

FOSDICK, DAVID, Jr.—A German-English and English-German Pocket Dictionary, &c.—8vo, Boston, 1847. (C.)

FREY, JOSEPH SAMUEL C. F.—Hebrew and English Dictionary, containing all the Hebrew and Chaldaic Words used in the Old Testament, arranged under one Alphabet; the derivations referred to their respective Roots, and their Signification in English, &c., &c.—8vo, London, 1839. (C.)

GREBO.—A Dictionary of the Grebo Language. Printed at the Press of the American Board of Commissioners of Foreign Missions.—4to, Fair Hope, (Cape Palmas,) Western Africa, 1839. (C.)

HERMANUS, J. G.—A Greek and German Wordbook, or Lexicon of the New Testament.—12mo, Frankfort on the Oder, 1781. (C.)

JOHNSON, SAMUEL, LL.D.—A Dictionary of the English Language.—2 vols. 4to, Philadelphia, 1819. (C.)

JOSEPH, P. ANGELO A S.—Gazophylaciane Linguae Persarum, Triplici Linguarum Clavi, Italicae, Latinae, Gallicae.—Fol., Amsterdam, 1684. (C.)

JUDSON, A.—A Dictionary of the Burman Language, with Explanations in English; compiled from the MSS. of A. Judson, D.D., and of other Missionaries in Burmah.—8vo, Calcutta, 1826. (C.)

KERSCHIUS, GULIELMO.—Lexicon Syriacum, Chrestomathiae Sare Syriacae accommodatum a M. Georgis.—12mo, Leipsic, 1789. (C.)

NEWMAN.—A Dictionary of the Spanish and English Languages, &c., &c. Fourth edition.—2 vols. 8vo, London, 1823. (C.)

NEWMAN.—A Dictionary of the Spanish and English Languages. Second American, from the fourth London edition.—2 vols. 8vo, Boston, 1827. (C.)

PASSOR, GEORGE.—A Greek and Latin Lexicon of the New Testament.—18mo, Frankfort, 1655. (C.)

Honourable mention is made of this Lexicon in Winer's Idioms of the Language of the New Testament. Also in Franke's Guide to the Study of the Holy Scriptures.

RICHARDSON, CHARLES.—A new Dictionary of the English Language.—2 vols. 4to, London, 1839. (C.)

ROY, W. L.—A complete Hebrew and English critical and pronouncing Dictionary, on a new and improved plan.—8vo, New York, 1837. (C.)

SCHAF, CAROLO.—Lexicon Syriacum Concordantiale omnes Novi Testamenti Syriaci voces et ad harum illustrationem multas aliis Syriacas, et Linguarum affinium dictiones complectens, &c., &c.—4to, Lugduni Batavorum, 1708. (C.)

SEWEL, W.—Groot Woordenboek, or Large Dictionary, English and Dutch, wherein each Language is set forth in its proper form; the various significations of the words being exactly noted, and abundance of choice Phrases and Proverbs intermixed. To which is added, a Grammar for both Languages.—4to, Amsterdam, 1749. (C.)

TAKOOR, MOHUNPERSAND.—A Vocabulary, Bengalee and English, for the use of Students.—8vo, Hindostan Press, Calcutta, 1810. (C.)

VIEYRA, ANTHONY.—A Dictionary of the Portuguese and English Languages, in two Parts: Portuguese and English, and English and Portuguese.—2 vols. 8vo, London, 1809. (C.)

VIEYRA, ANTHONY.—A new Pocket Dictionary, abridged from Vieyra, English and Portuguese, &c.—4to, London, 1809. (C.)

VIEYRA, ANTHONY.—Portuguese and English Dictionary, abridged from Vieyra, &c., by J. D. Do Canto.—16mo, London, 1826. (C.)

WEBSTER, NOAH, LL.D.—An American Dictionary of the English Language, &c.—4to, Springfield, 1848. (C.)

DICCIONARIO de la Lengua Castellana, por la Academia Española. Seventh edition.—4to, Madrid, 1823. (C.)

This is the standard Spanish Dictionary.

CONCORDANCES.

BROWN, REV. JOHN.—A Concordance to the Holy Scriptures, &c.—12mo, Brooklyn, 1812. (C.)

CRUDEN, ALEXANDER, A.M.—A complete Concordance to the Holy Scriptures, &c. Tenth edition.—8vo, London, 1825. (C.)

CRUDEN, ALEXANDER, A.M.—A complete Concordance to the Holy Scriptures, &c. Eleventh edition.—4to, London, 1848. (C.)

CRUTWELL, REV. C.—A Concordance of Parallels, collected from Bibles and Commentaries which have been published in Hebrew, Latin, French, Italian, Spanish, English, and other Languages, &c.—4to, London, 1790. (C.)

"This work may be useful for occasional consultation, but the references are often so numerous under a single verse that it is scarcely possible to examine them all, or to perceive the design of each." [Orme, in Lowndes' British Librarian, p. 85.]

TROMMIUS, ABRAHAM.—Volkomene Nederlansche Concordantie ofte Woord-Register des ouden Testaments; eerste Deel; vervaltewde alle de Historische boecken van Genesis af tot Esther incluys, &c., &c.—Fol., Amsterdam, 1685. (C.)

TROMMIUS, ABRAHAM.—Concordantiae Graecae Versionis Vulgo dictae LXX. Interpretum, &c., &c.—2 vols. fol., Amsterdam, 1718. (C.)

ENGLISH MISCELLANY.

ANDERSON, CHRISTOPHER.—The Annals of the English Bible.—2 vols. 8vo, 1845. (B.)

ANDERSON, RUFUS.—Observations upon the Peloponnesus and Greek Islands, made in 1829.—12mo, Boston. (B.)

BARCLAY, ROBERT.—An Apology for the true Christian Divinity; being an Explanation and Vindication of the Principles and Doctrines of the People called Quakers. Written in Latin and English.—8vo, New York, 1827. (B.)

BARNARD, HENRY.—A Discourse in Commemoration of the Life, Character, and Services of the Rev. Thomas H. Gallaudet, LL.D., delivered before the Citizens of Hartford, January 7, 1852, with an Appendix, containing a History of Deaf-mute Instruction and Institutions, and other Documents.—8vo, Hartford, 1854. (B.)

BARRINGTON, A.—A Treatise on Physical Geography, comprising Hydrology, Geology, &c., &c.—12mo, New York, 1850. Two copies. (B.)

BAXTER, RICHARD.—A Call to the Unconverted. Printed in Raised Letters at the New England Institution for the Education of the Blind.—4to, Boston, 1836. (B.)

BELLAMY, JOSEPH, D.D.—The Works of.—3 vols. 8vo, New York, 1811. (B.)

BELLAMY, J.—A Critical Examination of the Objections made to the New Translation of the Bible.—8vo, London, 1820. (B.)

BERRIMAN, JOHN, M.A.—A critical Dissertation upon 1 Tim., iii., 16, &c., with an Account of above one hundred Greek MSS. of St. Paul's Epistles, &c., and the common Reading of that Text proved to be the true one.—8vo, London, 1741. (B.)

BLACK.—A General Atlas: a Series of fifty-four Maps, from the latest and most authentic Sources. Engraved on Steel by Sydney Hall.—Fol., Edinburgh, 1841. (B.)

BLAKE, J. L., D.D.—A General Biographical Dictionary, comprising a summary Account of the most distinguished Persons of all Ages and Professions, &c. Second edition.—8vo, Philadelphia, 1840. (B.)

Blunt, Rev. J. J.—The designed Coincidences in the Writings both of the Old and New Testaments, an Argument of their Veracity, &c., &c.—8vo, New York, 1847. (B.)

Bonnycastle, J.—The Scholar's Guide to Arithmetic.—Philadelphia, 1818. (B.)

Brantley, William T., D.D.—Objections to a Baptist Version of the New Testament, &c.—12mo, New York, 1837. (B.)

Brett, Rev. H. W.—The Indian Tribes of Guiana.—12mo, New York, 1852. (B.)

Bridges, Rev. Charles.—A Memoir of Miss Mary Jane Graham, late of Stoke Fleming, Devo.—12mo, Boston and New York, 1834. (B.)

Broughton, Hugh.—The Works of the great Albionean Divine, renowned in many Nations for rare skill in Salems and Athens Tongues, and familiar acquaintance with all Ribbinical Learning, Mr. Hugh Broughton, collected in one Volume, and digested into four Tomes.—Fol., London, 1662. (B.)

Brown, William C.—The Wesleyan Harp, &c.—12mo, Boston, 1841. (B.)

Burder, Samuel.—An Illustration of the Sacred Scriptures from the Customs and Manners of the Eastern Nations, &c., &c.—8vo, London, 1802. (B.)

Bush, Rev. George.—Illustrations of the Holy Scriptures, derived principally from the Manners, Customs, &c., &c., of the Eastern Nations.—8vo, Brattleborough, 1836. Two copies. (B.)

Bush, Rev. George.—The Hierophant, or Monthly Journal of Sacred Symbols and Prophecy.—8vo, New York, 1835. (B.)

Calvin, John.—Institutes of the Christian Religion, with Mackenzie's Memoir of the Author. Dedicated to Francis, King of France.—4to. (B.)

This volume has no publisher's name, date, nor place of publication. The Translator's Preface is dated, London, 1813.

Campbell, Rev. A.—A Debate between Rev. A. Campbell and Rev. N. L. Rice, on the Action, Subject, Design, and Administration of Christian Baptism, &c., &c.—8vo, Lexington, (Ky.,) 1844. (B.)

Carpenter, William.—A Guide to the practical Reading of the Bible.—18mo, London, 1830. Two copies. (B.)

CAVE, WILLIAM, D.D.—The History of the Life and Death of the Holy Jesus, as also the Lives, Acts, and Martyrdoms of his Apostles. In two Parts. By Bishop Taylor and William Cave, D.D. Printed at the Angel, in Amen-corner.—Fol., 1675. (B.)

COGSWELL, WILLIAM, D.D.—The Christian Philanthropist, &c.—12mo, Boston, 1839. (B.)

COLBURN, WARREN.—Sequel to the Mental Arithmetic.—12mo, Boston, 1822. (B.)

COLEMAN, LYMAN.—The Antiquities of the Christian Church.—8vo, New York, 1846. (B.)

COTTON, REV. HENRY, D.C.L.—A List of the Editions of the Bible and Parts thereof in English, from the year 1505 to 1820, with Specimens of Translations, &c. (Interleaved.)—8vo, Oxford, 1821. (B.)

COVERDALE, MYLES.—Memorials of the Right Rev. Father in God, Myles Coverdale, who first translated the whole Bible into English, &c.—8vo, London, 1838. (B.)

CRANTZ, DAVID.—The History of Greenland, containing a Description of its Inhabitants, particularly with reference to the Mission of the United Brethren, &c. Illustrated with Maps and Plates.—2 vols. 12mo, London, 1768. (B.)

CRANTZ, DAVID.—A succinct Narrative of the Protestant Church of the United Brethren, Ancient and Modern, &c., &c. Translated into English by B. Latrobe.—8vo, London, 1780. (B.)

DARBY, WILLIAM.—A Universal Gazetteer.—8vo, 1845. (B.)

D'AUBIGNE, J. H. MERLE.—History of the great Reformation of the Sixteenth Century, &c. Fifth American edition.—4 vols. 12mo, New York, 1853. (B.)

DAVENPORT.—A Gazetteer or Geographical Dictionary of North America and the West Indies.—8vo, 1833. (B.)

DAVIS.—A History of Changes, Events, &c., in the United States, between 1800 and 1850. With an Introduction by Mark Hopkins, D.D.—12mo, Boston, 1851. (B.)

DAVIS, J. K.—The Seaman's and Boatman's Manual.—18mo, New York, 1847. (B.)

DEALTRY, WILLIAM.—A Vindication of the British and Foreign Bible Society, &c., in reply to Dr. Wordsworth's Letter to Lord Teignmouth.—8vo, London, 1810. (B.)

DICKINSON, RODOLPHUS.—A Compendium of the religious Doctrines, &c., and descriptive Beauties of the Bible, &c., &c.—18mo, Greenfield, (Mass.,) 1815. (B.)

DOGGETT.—The New York City Directory for 1843–44.—8vo, New York, 1843. (B.)

DOUGLASS, JAMES.—Advancement of Society in Knowledge and Religion. Second edition.—8vo, Edinburgh, 1828. (B.)

DOWNAME, JOHN.—A Treatise of a Christian Life.—Fol., London, 1622. (B.)

DUDLEY, C. S.—An Analysis of the System of the Bible Society, throughout its various Parts, &c., &c.—8vo, London, 1821. Three copies. (B.)

EBAUGH, JOHN S.—A newly opened Treasury of Heavenly Incense, &c.—8vo, Philadelphia, 1836. (B.)

In unreadable type, with a portrait of the author.

ELLESMERE, RT. HON. THE EARL OF.—A Guide to Northern Archaeology, by the Royal Society of Northern Antiquaries of Copenhagen.—8vo, London, 1848. (B.)

FINDLAY, ROBERT.—A Vindication of the Sacred Books and of Josephus, &c., from various Misrepresentations and Cavils of the celebrated M. de Voltaire.—8vo, Glasgow, 1770. (B.)

"A serious and solid refutation."—Bishop Watson.

FISHER, RICHARD S., M.D.—A new and complete Statistical Gazetteer of the United States of America, &c., &c.—8vo, New York, 1853. (B.)

FLINT, TIMOTHY.—The History and Geography of the Mississippi Valley, &c., &c. Second edition.—2 vols. 8vo, Cincinnati, 1832. (B.)

FOOTE, REV. WILLIAM HENRY.—Sketches of North Carolina, Historical and Biographical, illustrative of the Principles of a portion of her early Settlers.—8vo, New York, 1846. (B.)

GARDINER, MARY L.—Prose and Poetical Writings.—12mo, New York, 1843. Three copies. (B.)

GAUSSEN.—Theopneusty, or the Plenary Inspiration of the Holy Scriptures. Translated by E. N. Kirk.—12mo, New York, 1842. (B.)

GEDDES, REV. ALEXANDER, D.D.—Memoirs of the Life and Writings of.—8vo. Imperfect. (B.)

GELL, ROBERT.—An Essay toward the Amendment of the last English Translation of the Bible, &c., &c.—Fol., London, 1659. (B.)

GIUSTINIANI, REV. L., D.D.—Papal Rome as it is.—12mo, Baltimore, 1843. (B.)

GOODELL, WILLIAM.—The Old and the New; or, the Changes of Thirty Years in the East, with some Allusions to Oriental Customs as elucidating Scripture. With an Introduction by Rev. William Adams, D.D. —12mo, New York, 1853. (B.)

GREENLEAF, REV. JONATHAN.—Sketches of the Ecclesias tical History of the State of Maine, &c., &c.—12mo, Portsmouth, N. H., 1821. (B.)

GRIMSHAW, REV. T. S.—Memoir of Rev. Leigh Richmond. Sixth edition.—12mo, New York, 1830. (B.)

HAGER, JOSEPH, D.D.—An Explanation of the Elementary Character of the Chinese, with an Analysis of their ancient Symbols and Hieroglyphics.—4to, London, 1801. (C.)

HAMILTON, JAMES, D.D.—The Lamp and the Lantern; or, Light for the Tent and the Traveller.—18mo, New York, 1853. (B.)

HASKEL, DANIEL, A.M.—A complete Descriptive and Statistical Gazetteer of the United States of America, &c., with an Abstract of the Census, &c., for 1840.—8vo, New York, 1843. (B.)

HAWES, REV. JOEL.—Lectures on the Literary History of the Bible.—8vo, Hartford, 1833. (B.)

HAYNE.—The Times, Places, and Persons of the Holy Scriptures.—Fol., London, 1640. (B.)

HOWE, S. G.—The Reader; or, Extracts from English and American Authors, for the use of the Blind. Printed in Raised Letters.—4to, Boston, 1839. (B.)

HOWE, FISHER.—Travels in the East.—2 vols. 12mo, New York, 1854. (B.)

HOWEL, LAWRENCE.—A complete History of the Holy Bible, &c., &c., in which are inserted the occurrences that happened during the space of about four hundred years, from Malachi to Christ. Adorned with cuts. Sixth edition.—3 vols. 8vo, London, 1752. (B.)

JENKS, REV. WILLIAM, D.D.—The Explanatory Bible Atlas and Scripture Gazetteer, Geographical, Topographical, and Historical, &c., &c.—4to, Boston, 1847. (B.)

The best work of the kind in English.]

Johnson, Theodore T.—Lights in the Gold Region, and Scenes by the Way; with numerous Illustrations.—12mo, New York, 1850. (B.)

Jones, William.—The History of the Christian Church, from the Birth of Christ to the Eighteenth Century, &c.—2 vols. 8vo, New York, 1824. (B.)

Kennicott, Benjamin.—The State of the Hebrew Text of the Old Testament, considered in two Parts, &c., &c.—8vo, Oxford, 1753. (B.)

An important work.

Kennedy, John.—A complete System of Astronomical Chronology, &c., proving the Authenticity of the Masoretic Hebrew Text of the Holy Scriptures; fixing the Date of the Creation, the Exodus from Egypt, the Change of the Sabbath, &c., &c.—Fol., London, 1762. (B.)

King, Rev. David, LL.D.—The Principles of Geology, &c., in their Relations to Revealed and Natural Religion.—16mo, New York, 1851. (B.)

Kitto, John, D.D.—A Cyclopaedia of Biblical Literature, with numerous Engravings.—2 vols. 8vo, New York, 1846. (B.)

Knowles, James D.—Memoir of Mrs. Ann H. Judson, late Missionary to Burmah, &c.—12mo, Boston, 1829. (B.)

Layard, Austen Henry, Esq., D.C.L.—Nineveh and its Remains, &c., &c.—2 vols. 8vo, New York, 1849. (B.)

Lewis.—A complete History of the several Translations of the Holy Bible and New Testament into English, both in Manuscript and in Print, and of the most remarkable Editions of them since the Invention of Printing. Second edition.—8vo, London, 1739. (B.)

Livermore, George.—Remarks on Public Libraries, from the North American Review for July, 1850. Printed for private distribution.—8vo, Cambridge, 1850. (B.)

Livermore, George.—Remarks on the Publication and Circulation of the Holy Scriptures, suggested by Rev. W. P. Strickland's History of the American Bible Society. From the Christian Examiner of November, 1849.—8vo, Cambridge, 1849. (B.)

Loskiel, George Henry.—History of the Mission of the United Brethren among the Indians of North America. Translated from the German, &c.—8vo, London, 1794. (B.)

Mathews, J. M., D.D.—The Bible and Civil Government, in a Course of Lectures.—12mo, New York, 1850. (B.)

McClure, A. W.—A Biographical Memoir of the Authors of the English Version of the Holy Bible.—12mo, New York, 1853. (B.)

McCrie, Thomas, D.D.—History of the Progress and Suppression of the Reformation in Spain in the Sixteenth Century.—8vo, Edinburgh and London, 1829. (B.)

McGavin, William.—Essays on the Controversy between the Church of Rome and the Reformed, with an Appendix, &c., &c.—2 vols. 8vo, Hartford, 1853. (B.)

McIlvaine, Charles P., D.D.—The Evidences of Christianity in their External Division, &c., &c.—8vo, New York, 1832. (B.)

McLeod, Alexander, D.D.—The Larger Catechism, with Proofs, &c., revised.—12mo, New York, 1813. (B.)

The first book ever stereotyped in America.

Medhurst, W. H., Sen.—An Inquiry into the proper Mode of rendering the word "God" in Translating the Sacred Scriptures into the Chinese Language.—8vo, Shanghae, 1848. (B.)

Middleton, F. F., D.D.—The Doctrine of the Greek Article applied to the Criticism and Illustration of the New Testament.—8vo, New York, 1813. (B.)

Milner, Isaac, D.D.—Strictures on some of the Publications of Rev. Hebert Marsh, D.D., &c., against the British and Foreign Bible Society.—8vo, London, 1813. (B.)

Morse, Jedidiah, D.D., and Richard C., A.M.—The Traveller's Guide, &c., &c.—18mo, New Haven, 1823. (B.)

Morse, Jedidiah, D.D.—A new Universal Gazetteer, or Geographical Dictionary, &c., &c. Third edition.—8vo, New Haven and Hartford, 1821. (B.)

Mohammed.—See Koran, in *Foreign Miscellany*, (Anonymous.)

Newcomb, Rev. Harvey.—A Cyclopedia of Missions; containing a comprehensive View of Missionary Operations throughout the World, with Geographical Descriptions, and Accounts of the Social, Moral, and Religious Condition of the People.—8vo, New York, 1854. (B.)

Newcome, William, D.D.—An Historical View of English Biblical Translations, &c., with reference to a Revision of our present Translation.—8vo, Dublin, 1792. (B.)

Nolan, Rev. Frederic.—An Inquiry into the Integrity of the Greek Vulgate, or received Text of the New Testament.—8vo, London, 1815. (B.)

Norris, Rev. H. H.—Letter to the Earl of Liverpool respecting his Speech at a Bible Society Meeting, &c. Second edition.—8vo, London, 1823. (B.)

Norris, Rev. H.—A Practical Exposition of the Tendency and Proceedings of the British and Foreign Bible Society, &c., &c.—8vo, London, 1814. (B.)

O'Callaghan, E. B., M.D.—The Documentary History of the State of New York, &c.—4 vols. 4to, Albany, 1850. (B.)

Owen, Rev. John, A.M.—The History of the Origin and first ten Years of the British and Foreign Bible Society.—2 vols. 8vo, London, 1816. (B.)

This copy was presented by the author.

Owen, Rev. John, A.M.—History of the British and Foreign Bible Society, as above.—8vo, New York, 1817. (B.)

Owen, Rev. John, A.M.—History of the British and Foreign Bible Society, &c.—3 vols. 8vo, London, 1820. (B.)

Paley, William, D.D.—The Principles of Moral and Political Philosophy. Tenth edition.—8vo, Boston, 1821. (B.)

Pettigrew, Thomas.—A Descriptive Catalogue, &c., of the Library of the Duke of Sussex, in Kensington Palace.—2 vols. 8vo, London, 1827. (B.)

Plumer, W. S.—Lectures on the Evidences of Christianity, delivered at the University of Virginia during the Session of 1850-1—8vo, New York, 1852. (B.)

Porteus, Beilby, D.D.—Lectures on the Gospel by St. Matthew.—2 vols. 8vo, London, 1805. (B.)

Prettyman, George, D.D.—An Introduction to the Study of the Bible, &c., &c.—12mo, Philadelphia, 1806. (B.)

Rice.—See Campbell.

Roper, R. S. D., and Henry Hopley White.—A Treatise on the Law of Legacies. Second American edition.—2 vols. 8vo, Philadelphia, 1848. (B.)

Ross, Hugh.—An Essay for a new Translation of the Bible, &c., &c.—8vo, London, 1727. (B.)

A translation from a French work without acknowledgment.

Schoolcraft, Henry R., LL.D.—Information respecting the History, Condition, and Prospects of the Indian Tribes of the United States, collected and prepared under the direction of the Bureau of Indian Affairs, per Act of Congress March 3, 1847. Published by Authority of Congress.—4 vols. 4to, Philadelphia, 1854. (B.)

A most valuable contribution to the aboriginal History of our country.

SHARP, GRANVILLE.—Remarks on the Use of the Definitive Article in the Greek Text of the New Testament, &c., &c. Third edition.—12mo, London, 1803. (B.)

SMITH, CAPTAIN JOHN.—The true Travels, Adventures, and Observations of Captain John Smith, &c., from 1593 to 1629, with the History of Virginia, New England, &c., from 1584 to 1626, &c. From the London edition of 1629.—2 vols. 8vo, Richmond, 1819. (B.)

SMITH, J. V. C.—A Pilgrimage to Egypt, embracing a Diary of Explorations on the Nile, &c.—12mo, Boston, 1852. (B.)

SPAFFORD.—Gazetteer of the State of New York.—8vo, New York, 1813. (B.)

SPRING, GARDINER, D.D.—Christian Confidence illustrated in the Death of Rev. Edward D. Griffin.—18mo, New York, 1838. (B.)

STACKHOUSE, REV. THOMAS, A.M.—A History of the Holy Bible from the beginning of the World to the establishment of Christianity, &c.—2 vols. in 1, fol., London, 1787-8. (B.)

STONE, REV. JOHN S., D.D.—Memoir of the Life of James Milnor, D.D., late Rector of St. George's Church, New York.—8vo, New York, 1848. (B.)

STRAUCHIUS, GILES, D.D.—Breviarium Chronologicum; or, a Treatise describing the Terms and most celebrated Characters, Periods, and Epochas used in Chronology. Originally written by Giles Strauchius, D.D., &c., and first done into English from the third edition in Latin, by Richard Sault, F.R.S.—8vo, London, 1745. (B.)

STRICKLAND, WILLIAM P.—History of the American Bible Society from its Organization to the present time.—8vo, New York, 1845. (B.)

SYMONDS, JOHN, LL.D.—Observations upon the Expediency of revising the present English Version of the Four Gospels, and of the Acts of the Apostles.—4to, Cambridge, 1789. (B.)

TAYLOR.—See CAVE.

TODD, REV. HENRY JOHN, M.A.—A Vindication of our authorized Translation and Translators of the Bible, and of preceding English Versions, authoritatively commended to the notice of those Translators, &c.—8vo, London, 1819. (B.)

TOMLINSON, ROBERT, ESQ.—An Attempt to rescue the Holy Scriptures from the Ridicule they incur, &c., from incorrect Translation, by a new Translation of the controverted Passages, &c., &c.—8vo, London, 1805. (B.)

TONG, REV. WILLIAM.—An Account of the Life and Death of Mr. Matthew Henry, &c.—Fol., Edinburgh, 1767. (B.)

TRACY, E. C.—Memoir of the Life of Jeremiah Evarts, Esq., late Corresponding Secretary of the American Board of Commissioners for Foreign Missions.—8vo, Boston, 1845. (B.)

TURNER, SAMUEL H., D.D.—Essay on our Lord's Discourse at Capernaum, (John, vi.)—12mo, New York, 1845. (B.)

TURNER, SAMUEL H., D.D.—Biographical Notices of some of the most distinguished Jewish Rabbies, &c.—12mo, New York, 1847. (B.)

TWELLS, LEONARD.—A Critical Examination of the late new Text and Version of the New Testament, wherein the Editor's corrupt Text, false Version, and fallacious Notes, are detected and censured.—8vo, London, 1731. (B.)

This is an able review of Dr. Mace's edition of the New Testament. Both the Greek text and the English version are severely criticised.

WESTWOOD, J. O., F.L.S.—Palaeographia Sacra Pictoria; being a Series of Illustrations of the ancient Versions of the Bible, copied from Illuminated Manuscripts executed between the Fourth and Sixteenth Centuries. —4to, London, 1843-45. (B.)

A splendid collection of specimens of the labour, ingenuity, and taste employed in the ancient production of copies of the Holy Scriptures with the pen.

WHITE, HENRY HOPLEY.—See ROPER, R. S. D.

WILKS, REV. SAMUEL CHARLES, M.A.—The Bible Society Question, considered in a Series of Letters addressed to the Bishop of Salisbury. —8vo, London, 1832. (B.)

WILLIAMS.—The New York Annual Register.—12mo, New York, 1830. (B.)

WINES, E. C.—Commentaries on the Laws of the Ancient Hebrews, &c.—8vo, New York, 1853. (B.)

WISE, ISAAC M.—History of the Israelitish Nation, from Abraham to the present time. Derived from the original Sources.—Vol. 1, 8vo, Albany, 1854. (B.)

WYCKOFF, W. H.—The American Bible Society and the Baptists; or, Shall the whole Word of God be given to the Heathen? &c.—12mo, New York, 1842. (B.)

ANONYMOUS.

A Vindication of the Miracles of our blessed Saviour, &c. By the Lord Bishop of St. David's. Second edition.—8vo, London, 1729. (B.)

A Collection of Letters and Essays on the Antiquities of Great Britain and Ireland, &c.—8vo, Edinburgh, 1739. (B.)

Dissertation on the Characters and Sounds of the Chinese Language, &c.—4to, Serampore, 1809. (C.)

Russian Miscellanies.—8vo, 1815. (B.)

Archaeologia Americana; or, the Transactions and Collections of the American Antiquarian Society.—8vo, Worcester, 1820. (B.)

Archaeologia Americana; or, the Transactions and Collections of the American Antiquarian Society.—2 vols. 8vo, Cambridge, 1836. (B.)

Views in Theology; 1824 to 1827, vol. 1.—8vo, New York, 1824. (B.)

A Collection of Tracts, Essays, &c., on the Apocryphal Controversy.—8vo, 1822-26. (B.)

Memorial for the Bible Societies in Scotland, containing Remarks on the Complaint of His Majesty's Printers against the Marquis of Huntly and others. Printed by A. Balfour & Co. for the Edinburgh Bible Society.—12mo, Edinburgh, 1824. (B.)

The Book of Common Prayer, &c., &c.—18mo, London, 1825. (B.)

The Apocryphal New Testament, being all the Gospels, Epistles, and other Pieces now extant, attributed, in the first four Centuries, to Jesus, his Apostles, and their Companions, &c., &c. First American edition.—12mo, Philadelphia, 1825. (B.)

Specimens of the various Languages into which the Scriptures have been translated by the British and Foreign Bible Society.—2 vols. 4to, 1828 and 1833. (B.)

These volumes were presented by the British and Foreign Bible Society.

The Blind Child's Book. Printed at the New England Institution for the Blind. (In Raised Letters.)—12mo, Boston, 1835. (B.)

Sermons and Addresses.—8vo, 1836. (B.)

A Plan of the City of Athens.—1837. (B.)

An Accompaniment to Mitchell's Map of the World, &c., with the Map.—Philadelphia, 1837. (B.)

British and Foreign Bible Society Controversy, in a Series of Essays, &c.—4 vols. 8vo. (B.)

American Bible Society Controversy, in a Series of Essays, &c.—8vo. (B.)

Catalogue of the Books in the Library of the American Antiquarian Society.—8vo, Worcester, Mass., 1839. (B.)

A Gazetteer of the State of New York, &c., with the Census of 1840, and a new Map of the State.—8vo, Albany, 1842. (B.)

Constitution, &c., of the Cumberland Presbyterian Church. —18mo, Pittsburgh, 1843. (B.)

Constitution, Charter, &c., of the American Bible Society. 8vo, New York, 1845. (B.)

Psalms and Hymns, adapted to social, private, and public Worship in the Cumberland Church, &c.—24mo, Pittsburgh, 1845. (B.)

Questions to Lyman's Chart of History.—12mo, 1845. (B.)

American Tract Society's Publications.—7 vols. 12mo, Andover, 1850. (B.)

Manual of the Board of Education of the County and City of New York, with a Map of the City.—18mo, New York, 1850. (B.)

The Teachings of the Roman Catholic Church compared with the Bible. Printed by the American Tract Society.—18mo, New York, 1852. (B.)

The Liturgy; or, Forms of Divine Service of the French Protestant Church of Charleston, S. C., &c.—12mo, Charleston, 1853. (B.)

Tracts relating to Versions of the Scriptures.—8vo. (B.)

Catalogue of the Library of the British and Foreign Bible Society.—8vo, London, 1822. Pamphlet. (B.)

Guide to Northern Archaeology, by the Royal Society of Northern Antiquaries of Copenhagen. Edited by the Earl of Ellesmere.—8vo, London, 1848. Pamphlet. (B.)

Catalogue of Editions of the Holy Scriptures and other Biblical Works in the Library of the British and Foreign Bible Society.—8vo, London, 1832. Pamphlet. (B.)

MISCELLANY
IN FOREIGN LANGUAGES.

ALARDIN, CASPAR.—De geluksalighe van den weg der Rechtveerdig, &c., &c.; or, the Happiness of the Way of the Righteous; also, the Fountain of Life; being Sermons on Ps. i. and Ps. xxxvi., 8, 9, 10.—18mo, Arnheim, about 1700. (A.)

This copy is imperfect and without title page.

ARENDTS, JOHN.—Des eertyds Hoogverlichten Godgeleerden Heere Johan Arendts Alle VI. Geestryke Boeken van het Waare Christendom; or, the late highly enlightened Divine John Arendts' six Books on true Christianity, &c., &c.; translated from the German into Dutch, in German characters.—4to, Amsterdam, 1747. (B.)

ARIOSTO.—Orlando Furioso; with Memoirs and Notes by Antonio Panizzi.—12mo, London, 1834. (B.)

BALBI, ADRIAN.—Abrege de Geographie redige sur un nouveau plan d'apres les derniers traites de paix et les de convertes les plus recentes. Third edition, revised and enlarged by the author, and adopted by the University.—2 vols. 8vo, Paris, 1838. (B.)

BEELTSNYDER, JOHN.—Anathomie, dat is, Outledinge des Christelijcken Catechismi, &c.; or, the Dissection of the Christian (Heidelberg) Catechism, for the Confirmation of pure Doctrine, &c.—4to, Amsterdam, 1651. (B.)

BELTHUSEN, JOHN CASPAR.—German Homilies.—12mo, Helmstadt, 1783. (B.)

This copy is without title page, and imperfect.

BICKERSTETH.—Scripture Helps. Translated into Modern Greek.—Malta.

BRAKEL, THEODORE R.—The Degrees of the Spiritual Life.—12mo, Amsterdam, 1710. (A.)

BRAKEL, WILLIAM A.—Logike Latreia, dat is, Redelyke Godtsdienst, &c., &c.; or, reasonable Religious Service, in which the Divine Truths of the Covenant of Grace are defended and practically applied, &c. Seventeenth edition.—4 vols. 4to, Rotterdam, 1757. (A.)

BRAKEL, WILLIAM A.—Another copy of the above, the first two volumes in one.—4to. Imperfect. (A.)

BURNET, M.—Historie van de Reformatie der Kerke van Engeland; translated into English.—4to, Amsterdam, 1686. (A.)

CHRYSOSTOM, ST.—On the Reading of the Holy Scriptures, translated into Modern Greek.—12mo, Malta, 1832. (B.)

COSTERUS, FLORENCE.—Twee Predikatien; or, twelve Sermons.—18mo, Hoorn, about 1703. (A.)

The title page is wanting.

D'AUBIGNE, J. H. MERLE.—Historia de la Reformacion del Siglo Decimosecsto; traducida de la Cuarta Edicion Francesa, per Ramon Monsalvatge.—2 vols. 12mo, New York, 1850. (B.)

DE CASTRO.—See under ANONYMOUS.

DEURHOFF, WILLIAM.—Onderzoek van de Nootzaakelykheid en Onverschillendheid der Werkinge Gods; or, Letters and Essays in Dutch.—18mo, Amsterdam, about 1710. (B.)

DRELINCOURT, CHARLES.—Vertroostingen der gelovige ziele tegen de Verschrikkingen des Doodts, &c., &c.; or, the Consolations of the believing Soul against the fear of Death; translated into Dutch.—18mo, Amsterdam, 1741. (A.)

ELIOT, JOHN.—The Life and Labours of John Eliot, the Apostle of the American Indians, translated into Modern Greek.—12mo, Malta, 1831. (B.)

FOLSOM, CHARLES, A.M.—Titi Livii Pativini Historiarum Liber primus et selecta quaedam capita.—12mo, Boston, 1833. (B.)

FROHNIUS, D. JOH. ADOLPH.—Theologia Definitiva, comprehendens 1845 definitiones Theologicas, tam Theoreticas, quam Practicas, &c., rendered in German.—24mo, Molhusae, 1707. (B.)

GALLAUDET, T. H.—The Child's Book on the Soul, translated into Modern Greek. Part I.—12mo, Athens, 1838. (B.)

GALLAUDET, T. H.—The Youth's Book of Natural Theology, in Modern Greek.—12mo, Athens, 1840. (B.)

GALLAUDET, T. H.—The History of Josiah, in Modern Greek.—12mo, Athens, 1840. (B.)

GALLAUDET, T. H.—The Child's Book on Repentance, in Modern Greek.—12mo, Athens, 1840. (B.)

GALLAUDET, T. H.—The Child's Book on the Soul, in Modern Greek. Part II.—12mo, Athens, 1841. (B.)

HAPPES, ANDREW P.—A Compilation of Questions and Answers, on the Basis of Jacobus's Notes and Questions on Matthew.—8vo, 1853. (C.)

In Chinese characters.

HELLENBROEK, ABRAHAM.—Bybelsche Keurstoffen, &c., being Sermons on select Subjects from the Bible.—4to, Amsterdam, 1738. (A.)

KEITH, ALEXANDER, D.D.—The Evidences of Prophecy, derived from the Fulfillment of the Predictions of the Hebrew Prophets and the Apostles; translated into the Persian Language at Ooroomiah, by Rev. J. L. Merrick, Missionary, &c. Printed by the London Tract Society.—8vo, Edinburgh, 1846. (B.)

KNIBBE, DAVID.—Katechisatie over het Kort Begrijp, &c., &c.; or, a Catechism on the "Compendium" used in the Reformed Dutch Churches.—18mo, Leyden, 1760. (A.)

KOHLMAN, JACOB.—De Toetssteen van ons deel aan Christus, &c.; or, the Nature of true Piety exemplified in various Christian Experiences.—18mo, Amsterdam, 1680. (B.)

LAMPE, FREDERIC A.—Inley ding tot de Verborgentheid van het Genade Verbondt, &c.; or, an Introduction to his Work on the Covenant, with a Catechism.—18mo, Utrecht, 1723. Imperfect. (A.)

LAMPE, FREDERIC A.—Another old and imperfect copy of the above.—18mo. (B.)

LAMPE, FREDERIC A.—Two more copies of the same.—2 vols. 18mo, Amsterdam, 1779. (B.)

LAMPE, FREDERIC A.—A Catechism of the Christian Religion, &c., in Dutch.—18mo, Utrecht, 1721. (A.)

LAMPE, FREDERIC A.—Melk der Waarheit volgens aan leydinge van den Heidelbergschen-Catechismus, &c.; or, the Milk of Truth in the Order of the Heidelberg Catechism, for the Use of the Young.—18mo, Gravenhage, 1739. (B.)

LAMPE, FREDERIC A.—Another copy of the above.—18mo, Gravenhage, 1750. (B.)

LAMPE, FREDERIC A.—Another copy of the same, imperfect.—18mo, Gravenhage, 1750. (B.)

LAMPE, FREDERIC A.—De Verborgentheit van het Genaade Verbondt, &c.; or, the Secrets of the Covenant of Grace in the Economy of Salvation, &c.; translated into Dutch from the German.—18mo, Amsterdam, 1741. (B.)

LIEBERKUHN, REV. SAMUEL.—The History of our Lord and Saviour Jesus Christ, comprising all that the Evangelists have recorded concerning him, &c.; translated into the Delaware Indian Language.—12mo, New York, 1821. (A.)

MARK, JOHN.—Kort opstel der Christelijke Godgeleertheit, tot Leeringe der Waarheeden en Weederlegginge der Dwaalingen, getrokken uit de grootere Werken van Johannes a Marck, Leeraar, &c., tot Leyden, door Johannes Wilhelmius, S.T.D., &c., tot Rotterdam; or, a Compendium of Christian Theology, &c.; translated intò Dutch, by John Williams, S.T.D.—18mo, Rotterdam, about 1714. (B.)

MAYGOGEL, J. C.—An old volume of Dutch Poetry.—18mo, Amsterdam, (no date.) Imperfect. (B.)

MEL, CONRAD, S.T.D.—De geopende Genade-Throon, &c., &c.; or, the open Throne of Grace; choice Sermons before, at, and after the Lord's Supper, from the German.—4to, Amsterdam, 1751. (A.)

MEL, CONRAD, S.T.D.—De lust der Heiligen in Jehovah; or, the Delight of the Christian in God, &c.; a Book of Prayers, &c.—18mo, Amsterdam, 1760. Two copies. (B.)

OTTERBOS, LAURENS.—De geestelyke Mensch, voorgestelt, &c.; or, the Spiritual Man exhibited in the Ornaments of the various Christian Duties, as Fruits of the Spirit.—18mo, Amsterdam, 1727. (B.)

RIDDERUS, FRANCIS.—Historisch Sterf-Huys, &c.; or, the Historical House of Death for the Consolation of the Sick; being Accounts of the Sick and Dying, both from the World and the Church.—24mo, Amsterdam, 1678. (A.)

RIDDERUS, FRANCIS.—Dagelyksche Huys-Catechisatie, &c.; or, Daily Family Catechetical Instruction, being Exercises for Morning, Noon, and Evening.—12mo, Amsterdam, 1743. (B.)

RIEMEYER, DR. AUGUSTUS HERMAN.—History of the Canstein Biblical Institute from its Commencement to the present time, in German.—8vo, Halle, 1827. (B.)

ROEAFUERTE, VINCENT.—Lecciones para las escuelas de primeras letras, Sacadas de las Sagradas Escrituras, Liguendo el texto literal de la traduccion del Padre Scio, sui Notas ni Comentos. En tres partes; or, Lessons in Spanish, from the Sacred Scriptures, according to the Translation of Father Scio, without Note or Comment.—12mo, New York, 1823. (B.)

ROSS, J.—Catechismus Coetus Westmonasteriensis.—12mo, Philadelphia, 1813. (B.)

ROYAARDS, ALBERT.—De heerlykheid van Gods werken zoo in de Natuur als in de Genade, &c.; or, the Glory of God's Works of Nature and Grace, and the Excellency of his Law, explained and applied from Ps. xxi.—4to, Nymegen, 1728. (A.)

SALMON, THOMAS.—Hedendaagsche Historie of Tegenwoordige staat van alle volkeren, &c.; or, the present Statistics of all Nations. In two Parts, &c., &c. Translated into Dutch.—2 vols. 8vo, Amsterdam, 1736. (B.)

SCHORTINGHUIS, WILLIAM.—Het innige Christendom tot overtuiginge van onbegenadigde, &c., &c.; or, True Inward Religion exemplified in various Experiences and Conversations, for the Conviction of Unbelievers, &c.—4to, Groningen, 1752. (A.)

SIBERSMA, HERO.—Roem der Christenen in Christo Jesu, den Heere hare Geregtigheid, &c.; or, the glorying of Christians in Christ Jesus, the Lord their Righteousness, &c.—18mo, Leewaarden, 1687. (B.)

SIBERSMA, HERO.—Another copy, imperfect.—18mo. (A.)

SIBERSMA, HERO.—Fontein des Heils, aangewesen in den Heijdelbergsen Catechismus, &c.; or, the Fountain of Salvation, set forth in the Heidelburgh Catechism, more fully opened from the Scriptures.—4to, Leewaarden, 1703. (B.)

VAN ALPHEN, JEROME.—De voorseggingen van den Heere Jesus Christus aangaande de verwoesting van Jerusalem, &c., &c.; or, the Predictions of Christ respecting the Destruction of Jesuralem, &c., from Matt., xxiv. and xxv.—4to, Leewaarden, 1734. (A.)

VAN EENHOORN, WILLIAM.—Christelyke Jonkheit, waar in de Christelyke opvoeding van Kinderen, &c.; or, a Treatise on the Christian Education of Youth, &c. Part III.—8vo, Leewaarden, 1765. (B.)

VAN GRAVENBIGT, BALTHAZAR.—Een Kristen beproevd en verzeekerd; or, the Christian proved and established; a particular Treatise on Regeneration, &c.—18mo, Amersfoort, about 1714. (A.)

VAN DER HAGEN, PETER.—Verborgenheyt der Godsaligheyt; or, the Secret of true Piety, in three Parts, &c., &c., comprising 102 Sacramental Sermons on the History of Christ, &c.—4to, Amsterdam, 1686. (B.)

VAN LEEUWAARDEN, N. S.—The Christian Navigator.—18mo, Amsterdam, 1713. (B.)

VAN LODENSTEYN, J.—Geestelyke Opwekker voor het onverloochende Doode, en Geesteloose Christendom, &c.; or, the Spiritual Awakener of the Dead in lifeless Christendom, with a Memoir of the author. —12mo, Amsterdam, 1740. (A.)

VERMEER, JUSTUS.—De leere der Waarheid diena de Godtzaligheid, is; or, the Doctrine of Truth, which is according to Godliness, explained, &c., in LXXXV. Sermons on the Heidelberg Catechism.—4to Rotterdam, 1755. (B.)

The first part is wanting.

WITS, C. J.—Stigtelyke Bedenkinge, Ouledige Ledigbeid, Stigtelyke Tydkortinge, &c.; or, Religious Poems, &c.—18mo, Amsterdam, 1762. (B.)

There are also two other copies of the above, both of which are imperfect.

ZIEGENMEYR, JACOB.—De Wereldling outdekten tot een juychend Christen opgeleyd, &c.; or, the Worldling unmasked, and led to become a happy Christian, in six Dialogues, &c.—18mo, Amsterdam, 1750. (A.)

ANONYMOUS.

Christen Martelaers-Boek; or, the Book of Christian Martyrs, in Dutch, (German characters,) with numerous Illustrations.—Fol., Dort and Amsterdam, 1619. (A.)

A Defence of the Augsburg Confession of Faith, in German, by several Authors.—18mo, Leipsic, 1629. (B.)

Opuscula, Mythologica, Ethica et Physica, Graece et Latine.—8vo, Cambridge, 1671. (B.)

A German Liturgy, Catechism, &c.—18mo, Hamburgh, 1763. (B.)

De Aart der Volkeren, bevattende eene beschryving van het Karakter van de meeste Bewooneren der Waereld; or, the Character of the Nations of the Earth, &c., &c.—12mo, Leyden, 1766. (A.)

Psalms and Hymns, in Low Dutch, with a Liturgy for the Use of the Lutheran Congregations in the Netherlands.—12mo, Amsterdam, 1778. (B.)

Sanctorum Patrum, opera Polemica, de veritate Religionis Christianae, contra Gentiles et Judaeos; comprising the Works of Justin Martyr, Clemens Alexandrinus, Tertullian, Origen, Cyprian, Ambrose, Lactantius, and Hilary.—26 vols. 12mo, Wirceburgi, 1777-1785. (C.)

The Campaign in Prussia under Napoleon I. in 1806–7; translated into the Turkish Language.—4to. (B.)

Address du Comite aux Chretiens evangeliques de France, sur l'etablissement de Societes Auxiliaires; du Catalogue des Bible et Nouveaux Testamens, qui le trovent dans les Magasins de la Societe a Paris, Toulouse, Nismes, et Bordeaux.—4to, Paris, 1821. (B.)

Breviarum Romanum.—12mo, Venice, 1823. (B.)

Elementary Geography, in Modern Greek, with Plates.——12mo, 1835. (B.)

Repository of Useful Knowledge, a Newspaper, in Modern Greek. Vol. I., No. 11, Nov. 1, 1837.—4to, Smyrna. (A.)

Repository of Useful Knowledge, &c., as above, from 1839 to 1843.—2 vols. 4to, Smyrna. (A.)

Methodist Hymns, in the *Ojibwa* Language. Third edition. Printed by the American Tract Society.—24mo, New York, 1837. (B.)

A Harmony of the Gospels, in Modern Greek.—8vo, Hermopolis, 1837. (B.)

A short Account, in Modern Greek, of the Objects and Labours of the British and Foreign Bible Society, and of other Bible Societies; translated from the English.—8vo, Athens, 1838. (B.)

The Armenian Reader; published under the auspices of the American Board of Commissioners for Foreign Missions.—12mo, Smyrna, 1838. (B.)

The History of Abraham, in Modern Greek.—12mo, Athens, 1838. (B.)

The Lives of the Patriarchs, in Modern Armenian. Press of the American Board of Commissioners for Foreign Missions.—12mo, Smyrna, 1838. (B.)

Scripture Lessons, in Chinese.—3 vols. 8vo. Pamphlet. (A.)

A Romish Breviary.—12mo, Lugani, 1840. (B.)

The Pilgrim's Progress, in Modern Armenian; translated under the direction of the American Board of Commissioners for Foreign Missions.—12mo, Smyrna, 1843. (B.)

An Inquiry concerning the true Religion, &c.; translated into the Hindui Language from the Urdii. Presbyterian Mission Press.—12mo, Allahabad, 1844. (B.)

Al Koran; or, the Mohammedan Bible, in Arabic, with a running Commentary between the Lines. Lithographed from the best MSS. at the expense of a wealthy Mohammedan Merchant.—Fol., Bombay, 1848. (B.)

Al Koran; or, the Mohammedan Bible, without the Commentary.—8vo, Bombay, 1848. (B.)

The last Chapter of the Koran, in Arabic, for separate use. —8vo, Bombay, 1848. Pamphlet. (B.)

An old Volume in Dutch, on the Inspiration of the Scriptures. Without title page, and mutilated.—18mo. (B.)

A German Prayer Book. Defective.—12mo. (B.)

A remnant of an old Lutheran Prayer Book, in German. —18mo. (B.)

An old Volume in Dutch on the Types of the Old Testament. Imperfect.—18mo. (B.)

A Jewish Prayer Book, in Hebrew, with Hebrew-German Notes. Defective.—4to. (A.)

A Jewish Liturgy, in Hebrew. Imperfect.—32mo. (B.)

A Tract in the Chinese Language.—12mo. Pamphlet. (D.)

Reasons why I am not a Roman Catholic. A Pamphlet in the Syriac Language.—8vo. (H.)

Den Donder-Slagh der Godloosen, mit de Hemelsche Vreugde voor de geloovige Zielen; or, a Thunderbolt for the Ungodly; to which is added, The heavenly Peace of believing Souls.—24mo. (A.)

Imperfect. Title page gone.

Historia de los Protestantes Espanoles y de su persecucion por Felipe II., Escrita por Adolfo de Castro.—8vo, Cadiz, 1851. Pamphlet. (A.)

A Hebrew-German (or Patois) Paraphrase on the Pentateuch, the Megilloth, and the Haphtoran; designed for the Daughters of Israël, and those who are not conversant with the Hebrew. Written by Rabbi Jacob, Ben Isaac, of Janova, Lithuania.—4to, Sulzbach, 1730. (C.)

Imperfect in the latter part of the work.

A Treatise on Christian Faith and Practice, in the Siamese Language.—8vo, Bangkok. (A.)

Machzor, or a Collection of Prayers, according to the Ritual of the German-Jewish Congregations. Written in Hebrew and Hebrew-German or Patois. Vol. II. only.—4to, Wilhelmsdorf, 1738. (A.)

Christian Almanac for the Year 1853, in Chinese characters, published by order of the new Dynasty.—12mo. (B.)

Almanac of Peace for the Year 1853, in Chinese characters.—12mo. (B.)

REPORTS AND PERIODICALS.

Reports of the British and Foreign Bible Society from 1805 to 1815 inclusive.—3 vols. 8vo, London. Two copies. (J.)

Reports of the British and Foreign Bible Society from 1805 to 1817 inclusive.—5 vols. 8vo, London. Two copies. (J.)

Reports of the British and Foreign Bible Society from 1805 to 1816 inclusive.—5 vols. 8vo, London. (J.)

Reports of the British and Foreign Bible Society from 1805 to 1816 inclusive.—4 vols. 8vo, London. (J.)

Report of the British and Foreign Bible Society for the Year 1816.—8vo, London. Two copies. (J.)

Reports of the British and Foreign Bible Society from 1812 to 1840 inclusive, (with duplicate of 1818.)—16 vols. 8vo, London. (J.)

"Monthly Extracts" of the British and Foreign Bible Society from Nov. 30, 1821, to Nov. 29, 1828, inclusive.—8vo, London. (J.)

"Monthly Extracts" of the British and Foreign Bible Society from 1829 to 1848 inclusive.—2 vols. 8vo, London. (J.)

A book in the Russian Language, supposed to be Reports of Bible Societies.—8vo, St. Petersburgh, 1815. (J.)

Reports of the American Bible Society from 1816 to 1838 inclusive.—8vo, New York. (K.)

Reports of the American Bible Society from 1839 to 1843 inclusive. Volume II.—8vo, New York. (K.)

Reports of the American Bible Society from 1817 to 1820 inclusive.—8vo, New York. Two copies. (K.)

Reports of the American Bible Society from 1817 to 1826 inclusive.—2 vols. 8vo, New York. (K.)

Reports of the American Bible Society from 1821 to 1823 inclusive.—8vo, New York. (K.)

Reports of the American Bible Society from 1824 to 1827 inclusive.—8vo, New York. (K.)

Reports of the American Bible Society from 1832 to 1839 inclusive.—2 vols. 8vo, New York. (K.)

Reports of the American Bible Society, Nos. 1 to 15 inclusive.—3 vols. 8vo, New York. (K.)

Reports of the American Bible Society, Nos. 16 to 21 inclusive. Volume IV.—8vo, New York. (K.)

"Monthly Extracts" of the American Bible Society from 1821 to 1849 inclusive.—2 vols. 8vo, New York. (K.)

"Monthly Extracts" of the American Bible Society from May, 1823, to February, 1830, inclusive.—8vo, New York. (K.)

Reports of the New York Bible Society from 1834 to 1844 inclusive, except 1838.—8vo, New York. (J.)

Reports of Forty American Bible Societies from 1809 to 1814 inclusive.—8vo. (K.)

Reports of various Bible Societies in the United States for the Years 1809 to 1817 inclusive.—4 vols. 8vo. (K.)

Reports of the American and Foreign Bible Society from 1837 to 1847 inclusive.—8vo, New York. (J.)

Reports of the Hibernian Bible Society from 1806 to 1829 inclusive.—3 vols. 8vo. (J.)

"Monthly Extracts" of the Hibernian Bible Society from November 30, 1818, to April 30, 1821, inclusive.—4to, Dublin. (J.)

"Monthly Extracts" of the Hibernian Bible Society from May, 1821, to August, 1829, inclusive.—2 vols. 8vo. (J.)

Reports of the Swedish Bible Society from 1815 to 1819 inclusive.—2 vols. 8vo. (K.)

Reports of the Swedish Bible Society from 1820 to 1824 inclusive, (duplicates.)—2 vols. 8vo. (K.)

Reports of the Swedish Bible Society from 1825 to 1829 inclusive.—8vo. (K.)

Reports of the Swedish Bible Society from 1830 to 1834 inclusive.—2 vols. 8vo. (K.)

Reports of the Swedish Bible Society from 1835 to 1839 inclusive.—8vo, Stockholm. (K.)

Report of the Swedish Bible Society for 1833.—8vo, Stockholm, 1834. (K.)

The first ten Annual Reports of the American Board of Commissioners for Foreign Missions, with other Documents of the Board.—8vo, Boston, 1834. (K.)

Annual Reports of the American Board of Commissioners for Foreign Missions for the Years 1812 to 1833 inclusive.—3 vols. 8vo, Boston. (K.)

The Missionary Herald for the Year 1822. Vol. XVIII. —8vo, Boston. (K.)

The Missionary Herald for the Year 1823.—8vo, Boston. (K.)

The Missionary Herald for the Years 1828 to 1836 inclusive.—9 vols. 8vo, Boston. (K.)

The Massachusetts Register and United States Calendar for 1828.—18mo, Boston. (K.)

The Eclectic Review. Vol. IX., third Series.—8vo, London, 1833. (K.)

The Biennial Register of all Officers and Agents in the Service of the United States, &c.—12mo, Washington, D. C., 1838. (K.)

Transactions of the seventh Annual Meeting of the Western Literary Institute and College of Professional Teachers. Vol. IV.—8vo, Cincinnati, 1838. (K.)

The American Quarterly Register, (irregular.)—4 vols. 8vo, Boston. (K.)

The Foreign Missionary Chronicle for the Years 1833 to 1838 inclusive.—3 vols. 8vo, New York. (K.)

Report of the Light House Board to Congress.—8vo, Washington, 1852. (K.)

The Chinese Repository. Vols. III. to XIX. inclusive.— 17 vols. 8vo, Canton, 1834 to 1850. (K.)

Memoires de la Societe Royale des Antiquaires du Nord. —8vo, Copenhagen, 1844. Pamphlet. (K.)

Memoires de la Societe Royale des Antiquaires du Nord for the Years 1845 to 1849 inclusive.—8vo, Copenhagen. Pamphlet. (K.)

Message and Documents, twenty-ninth Congress of the United States, second Session.—8vo, Washington, 1846. Pamphlet. (K.)

Journal of the American Oriental Society, (Nos. 1 and 2 of the third volume.)—2 vols. 8vo, New York, 1852-3. Pamphlet. (K.)

The True Baptist, &c., edited by A. Newton. Vol. I., 1853.—8vo, Jackson, Miss., 1853. (K.)

Journal of the American Oriental Society. Vol. IV., No. II.—8vo, New York, 1854.

www.ingramcontent.com/pod-product-compliance
Lightning Source LLC
La Vergne TN
LVHW021425110826
845150LV00007B/2082

* 9 7 8 1 4 2 5 5 0 8 8 2 1 *